A GROUP STUDY BOOK

RENEW MY CHURCH

DAVID HANEY

ZONDERVAN PUBLISHING HOUSE   OF THE ZONDERVAN CORPORATION
GRAND RAPIDS, MICHIGAN 49506

RENEW MY CHURCH!
© 1972 by David P. Haney

Tenth printing 1980
ISBN 0-310-25871-5

Library of Congress Catalog Card Number 76-187964

Acknowledgments:
Quotations from *The New English Bible*, © 1961, 1970 by the Dele-
gates of the Oxford University Press and the Syndics of the Cambridge
University Press. Used by permission.

Quotations from *The Living Bible*, copyright © 1971 by Tyndale
House Publishers. Used by permission.

Quotations from The Revised Standard Version, New Testament section,
copyright © 1946, 1952 by Division of Christian Education of the
National Council of Churches of Christ in the United States of America.
Used by permission of the Division of Christian Education, National
Council of Churches. Zondervan Publishing House, Licensee.

Printed in the United States of America

To Dad

The Rev. George G. Haney

*"He loved the Church and gave
himself for it."*

Contents

FOREWORD

The Renewal Movement, which is the most hopeful Christian development of our generation, has arisen as a viable alternative to both apathy and despair. It is espoused by those who, in their loyalty to the Christian cause, reject both optimism and pessimism. They reject optimism because they recognize much in the Christian Church of which they are ashamed; they reject pessimism because they believe that improvement is possible. Like Charles Dickens when he wrote the opening lines of *A Tale of Two Cities*, they know that ours is both a bright time and a dark time, and they recognize that it is always a mistake to mention one without also mentioning the other.

The theological foundations of Renewal were soundly constructed shortly before the middle of the present century, with the conscious recovery of the doctrine of the Church. Leader after leader began, then, to see and to say that it is impossible to be an individual Christian. Earlier, the dictum of Professor Whitehead that religion is what a man does with his solitariness was accepted uncritically by thousands and repeated from numerous pulpits. When I heard the Lowell Lectures in which the widely quoted definition was uttered, I realized that I was listening to a very great man but, before many years had passed, I also saw that, at one important point, the great man was terribly wrong. Though there may be religions in which solitude is sufficient, the whole character of the Christian faith is of a totally different nature.

In future generations it is likely that historians of Christianity will see the recovery of the idea of the necessity of the Church as one of the major intellectual developments of the twentieth century. By the middle of the century, the old joke about believing in Christianity but not believing in Churchianity had already grown stale. It finally became clear that the man who said he believed in Christ but not in the Church was simply a confused person. And it was clear that he was confused because so much of the teaching of Christ is about the redemptive fellowship. Christ was not providing a message for a hermit living alone in the desert, but for men and women who gather to gain strength and who scatter to serve mankind. It was not to one alone, but to two or three together that He promised His presence. Even the early missionaries whom our Lord sent out, went out not one by one, but two by two in teams.

A major development came in my own mentality when I first saw that most of the New Testament revolved about the fellowship. One of the men who first made me see this was Charles Clayton Morrison, then editor of the *Christian Century* who published, in 1940, his Beecher Lectures in a book called *What Is Christianity?* Morrison's vivid observation was that the Christian fellowship, rather than being incidental to the revelation, was intrinsic to it. "The revelation," he said, "was not first given and afterward a community created to proclaim it. The creation of the community was itself the revelation of the activity of God."

The first literary result of the new insight in my own life was the writing of the Scarbrough Lectures, delivered at Austin, Texas, early in 1948. These lectures were published with the title, *Alternative to Futility*. The writing of this book was performed with a sense, on my part, of feverish excitement, because much of the renewal dream had suddenly burst upon me. I was greatly pleased, of course, when the phrase "The Fellowship of the Concerned" was adopted by groups devoted to renewal, regardless of denominational affiliations. It came to me as a fresh idea that the Church of Jesus Christ is meant to be a redemptive fellowship, in the sense that it is trying to save, not itself, but the world. As separate thinkers came independently to this general emphasis on the necessity of the Church, the ground of renewal was established. The more clearly we saw the ineptitude of our contemporary ecclesiastical establishments, the better. We had an incentive not for destruction, but for recovery. We saw that it is equally disloyal to Christ to be satisfied or to settle for no Church. If the Church is a permanent necessity for civilization and if the present forms of the Church are inadequate, then renewal is the only logical conclusion.

The hope that renewal is possible arises from the historical realism of any student who sees that new life has, in fact, emerged in many different periods. The biblical basis of this hope goes back to the Hebrew Scriptures and is given its most vivid expression in Ezekiel 37:1-14, in the parable of the Valley of Dry Bones. This parable epitomizes the pregnant combination of realism and hope, which must always be the stance of the people of God. What is really encouraging is that the parable has been enacted, over and over, in historical fact. Just when the darkness has seemed impenetrable, new light has shined, generation after generation. Renewal is therefore based upon the universalized philosophy of resurrection.

Once the idea of Renewal began to take hold of Christian minds, it replaced, in large measure, the interest in ecumenicity which preceded it. Many became convinced that there is no magic in union, whereas new life can be effective, even if denominational affiliations continue. Consequently, there are few today who are as excited as they once were by the ecumenical idea, while there is an increasing number, particularly of laymen, who are dedicated to what Robert Raines calls "New Life in the Church." Even the Vatican Council, advertised as an Ecumenical Council, was, in fact, devoted far more to Church Renewal than to Church Union.

There has been much to discourage us during the last twenty-five years, but the faith which keeps us going is centered in the conviction that new shoots can come from the old stump. That this is not mere speculation is shown by the fact that new life has actually appeared in several places. It is part of the merit of this volume that it draws attention to actual demonstrations of new life.

David P. Haney represents what may rightly be termed a new chapter in the Renewal Movement. Now as an active pastor, he sees the movement with a quarter century of experience behind it. For this reason, like others in the second generation, he does not need to engage in the elaboration of theory, but can proceed at once to practice. Accepting the validity of the argument, and especially the part which holds that there can be no renewal without the glad acceptance of the universal ministry, David Haney undertakes to show how to draw ordinary lay women and men into the active ministry of Christ. He understands, thoroughly, that we cannot have a universal ministry of mothers and businessmen simply by announcing it. This key step of renewal will not come to pass unless someone works at it, and pastors are the ones who are most free to give themselves to this holy task. This is the equipping ministry.

I welcome David Haney's book because it seeks deliberately to draw the more evangelical wing of the Christian movement into the concern for renewal. Up to now, there has been less interest among strong evangelicals in the development of small groups and in the cultivation of the universal ministry than there has been among those of liberal tendencies. This has been true partly because a great many evangelicals have depended, primarily, on mass evangelism. Now, however, they see that this is insufficient alone. Out of a sense of comparative failure, thoughtful Christians turn to new and promising ways of operation.

It is my hope that David Haney, by writing this book, may be able to reach a whole new sector of the general Christian community. If his book can introduce new readers to the work of Thomas Mullen, Keith Miller, and Elizabeth O'Connor, this will represent sheer gain. If people have not heard of the remarkable renewal which has occurred in an established congregation at Lancaster, Pennsylvania, I urge them to read the heartening account *From Tradition to Mission*, by Wallace Fisher. If there are discouraged Christians who have not yet encountered the mind of Keith Miller in *The Taste of New Wine*, I thank God that David Haney's book may turn them in this direction.

We need to be constantly alert to make sure that our contemporary emphasis is appropriate. What is needed at one period may not be needed, or may be actually harmful, at another period. Thus, there was a time when it was necessary to stress the present inadequacy of the churches, in order to shock people out of complacency. But that time is already gone, and now we need to share in the ministry of encouragement. People know how inadequate the Church of today is, and now they require hope concerning what it may again become. We need to say over and over in this particular generation that, however bad the Church may be, the alternative of a Churchless world is manifestly worse. And we need also to show that the emergence of new life in previous dark times makes it reasonable to expect the emergence of new life now.

It is too easy simply to attack the Church, and those who engage in this sport often end by being shallowly censorious. The Church is always vulnerable to criticism, because it provides, in the Gospel which it perpetrates, the materials for its own criticism. The Christian will always seem hypocritical for the simple reason that his standard, the standard of Christ, is higher than any man can reach. But calling attention to the failings of other people is an unlovely experience at best. One of the greatest dangers of our generation is that we are too moral in the sense that we call attention, with boring repetition, to the immorality of others. We are too judgmental! The time has come when we should stop judging the Church and begin reforming it. That is what the present book is about. I commend the work of my student to potential readers.

D. ELTON TRUEBLOOD

INTRODUCTION

> *We do not have to wait until we know the whole truth about anything to make our witness.*

What is *Renew My Church!* all about? Obviously, it is about the renewal of institutional Christianity. But, of course, there is more. It seeks to assess our present problems in the local church and to provide some *directions*—not *answers*. And this has determined its format.

The common problems we face and the directions in which renewal is to be found are given here only in "germ" form. Deliberately. The book's purpose is to excite (or incite) thought and discussion. No trails are blazed herein; it only points to potential paths. This sense of incompleteness will sometimes be frustrating, but even out of that very frustration may come an answer. Inevitably, the answers to renewal must be personal and local, whether it be an individual believer or a local church. Thus, no complete plans are given, plans which could be accepted or rejected *en toto*. Only possibilities are raised—which must be discussed and analyzed first, before acceptance or rejection can be made.

Renew My Church! is designed for any small group, but with an emphasis on the retreat setting. The chapters are brief and the book is short, allowing it to be covered during a retreat with no time problems, and allowing for ample discussion to emerge. It may also be used in small study groups, organized classes, or in individual study. Because it is a study book, as opposed to an essay, the skeletal structure is laid bare and, consequently, made easy to follow.

The reader will recognize the writer's indebtedness to Elton Trueblood. Dr. Trueblood stands at the very headwaters of Church Renewal; anyone who speaks or writes on the subject is his immediate debtor. This indebtedness is intensified for me in that I was his student at the Earlham School of Religion in Richmond, Indiana. The epigraphs which introduce each chapter are drawn from his many writings and serve to underscore the truth that he is America's most quoted (and quotable) religious author. He is also one of the Church's most discerning viewers, as well.

Not quite as obvious are two other debts: first, to the Yokefellow Group of the Heritage Baptist Church in Annapolis, Maryland, where it has been my happy assignment to serve as pastor since 1967. Most of the ideas projected in *Renew My Church!* have been tested against their insight and activity. Second, each year Dr. Trueblood invites a continuing group of former students and friends, along with an additional new set of participants, to an unprogrammed retreat on renewal at Lake Paupac in the Pocono Mountains. Whatever ideas are contained herein have been honed and sharpened by their tough minds and tender hearts.

Gratitude must be expressed to Joan Myers, my secretary, for typing the manuscript; to my wife, Aileen, for reading and correcting it; and to my associate, Willard G. Wild, who assumed many of my duties while it was being written.

Finally, the inspiration to put these ideas into words came from Ralph W. Neighbour, Jr., leader of the experimental West Memorial Baptist Church in Houston and the Director of the Evangelism Research Foundation. The small group creative procedures at the end of each chapter are his and reflect the incisiveness which has characterized all of his creative ministry. Since the purpose of this book is discussion, these procedures are to be taken seriously.

More and more evidence is on hand to reveal the Spirit's renewing work in our time. And more and more of Christ's followers are being lured into the deeper ways He is offering. Ultimately, then, *Renew My Church!* is for them. Perhaps it can provide a handle for someone's grasp in the new directions. Such is my prayer.

DAVID P. HANEY

Pastor's Study
Annapolis, Maryland

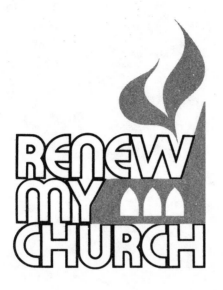

Chapter One

A BASIC ASSUMPTION

The Church of Jesus Christ, with all its blemishes, its divisions, and its failures, remains our best hope of spiritual vitality. However poor it is, life without it is worse.

The basic assumption of renewal is . . . the need. While for some the need is a foregone conclusion, the "business-as-usual" pace of the great masses within the churches indicates that it is not a universal conclusion. But, whether all are aware or not, the need is there. And, Step One on the way home is the admission on our part that . . .

THE CHURCH IS IN TROUBLE. While this may be "news" to some, it is not "new"; in a sense, the Church has always been in trouble. William Russell Maltby has so strikingly reminded us that Jesus promised those who would follow Him only three things: that they would be "absurdly happy, entirely fearless, and *always in trouble!*" Trouble is not new. But the kind and the degree of it is. And the point of evidence is obviously that of . . . effectiveness.

The seeds of the present problems have been with us for a while. The more discerning viewers saw it sometime ago. Over a decade ago, Elton Trueblood warned that our marks of success were superficial at best and that they were obscuring far deeper spiritual problems. The superficial marks of success to which he had reference were *growing memberships, increased attendance, financial growth,* and the *building expansions* of many congregations.[1] Karl Heim saw it also and wrote:

> The Church is like a ship on whose deck festivities are still kept up and glorious music is heard, while deep below the waterline a leak has been sprung and masses of water are pouring in, so that the vessel is settling hourly lower though the pumps are manned day and night.[2]

But *now*—even the superficial marks of success are disappearing! Banner headlines in all religious journals, whether denominational, ecumenical, or local, are decrying the losses in every area of church life. Membership is done. Attendance is down. Financial receipts are down. Baptisms are down. Educational organizations are losing members. Incident after incident of cutbacks in programs and personnel can be cited in every major religious enterprise.

As the superficial marks of success began to fade, other and more frightening problems were exposed. Today, as never before, *division* is apparent. Perhaps it has been there all along, but whether it has or not, it is there now. The division is not Catholic-Protestant, Baptist-Methodist, or even clergy-laity; in fact, the rift cuts across all of our former battle lines. It is dividing *within* the camps now: the *activists* over against the *pietists*. The focus of one is *society,* the other is *personal.* Agendas of all religious groups, from the local congregation to the World Council of Churches, grapple with it at every meeting. No group seems to be exempt from it and, tragically, all are losers—for the Christian Mission includes both!

Added to the problem of division is the problem of *deser-*

tion: the ministerial "drop-out" problem. While the ministerial shortage seems to be temporarily abated in that seminary
enrollments are up again, the rise is inconsequential in light
of the population increases. And, the *defection* from the ministry continues. Organizations now exist to aid former clergy-
men from *all* denominations to relocate in secular positions.
The almost universal reason given is that the organized
Church is without hope of recovery. More and more are
leaving, and fewer and fewer are entering! And of the few
who are entering, one professor, who had recently moved
from a college religion department to a seminary, observed
that the best college students were not the ministerial candi-
dates—and that the best seminary students were those totally
uninterested in the pastorate!

As one views Christianity *vis-a-vis* the world, there is far
more on the positive side than the negative, but the charges
and accusations are nonetheless evident. *Inconsistency!* That
is, there is an obvious and widening chasm between the
Church's claims and its ability to produce. One manifest
area of inconsistency is that of brotherhood. While we ought
to have been leading the parade against racial prejudice,
which cuts across all that Christ ever taught, we were, as
one sadly noted, "running a poor third to the U. S. Army
and the Brooklyn Dodgers." Indeed, the *strongest bastion* of
segregation was in the so-called "Bible Belt" and the *last
bastion* of segregation, in both the North and the South, is
. . . the local church!

Another charge is that of . . . *Irrelevancy!* "They" say, and
who can refute the charge, that the Church is concerned
with *programs*, not *people*, and that even the programs are
irrelevant! No one has focused more forcefully on contemporary Christianity's irrelevancy than Colin Morris. While serving as a missionary in Zambia, Morris reported that a native
was found dead not a hundred yards from the missionary
compound. The pathologist said he had died of starvation.
In his stomach were a few leaves and what appeared to be
a ball of grass. Meanwhile, back at home base, the current
"crisis" within his sponsoring denomination was . . . what

to do with the unused Bread after Communion! He continues, "You *can* die of Paul's assertion that women should wear
hats in Church but all the blood and fire and anguish will
not redeem the issue from triviality"![3]

Inability. The tide of secularism is rushing in upon our
world, and it exposes Christianity's inability and powerless-
ness as vividly as is possible. Secularism ("life without any
reference to God" as Rufus Jones defined it) charges that
Christianity is "past and gone" and seems to have some evidence on hand to verify it. It has given us a new morality, a
new value system, a new exaltation of science and its ability,
a new attitude of care-less-ness except for excitement (in a
sensual connotation) and a new philosophy. It makes no
difference as to secularity's shape, the "hippies" on one ex-
treme and the "materialists" on the other—the Church's
voice crying in the wilderness is but a whisper unheard and
lost in the wind. We have been able to convince them that
God is not dead, but all of us know that His Church is
severely wounded.

Isolation is another manifestation of the problem. Slowly,
but with increasing momentum, the institutional church has
isolated itself from the culture it was called to redeem! As
Elton Trueblood has pointed out, we have isolated ourselves
geographically—to a particular place, the Church building;
temporally—to a particular time, eleven o'clock on Sunday
morning; and in *personnel*—by limiting responsibility to the
professional clergy.[4] Consequently, we are not *where* the
people are, *when* the people are where they are, nor with
the right persons to meet them. The compounded result is
that we have lost contact with great segments of the population.

Finally, the problem is seen in Christianity's sometime . . .
Inanity! Just recently, a State Denominational Board spent
one hour and seventeen minutes on one single issue. It required motions, substitute motions, amendments, a lunch
break and five ballots to resolve. The "issue"? Whether or
not to allow wearing apparel at the denominational camp to
exceed more than four inches above the middle of the knee

cap! Fear was expressed that if the youth "won this battle," next year they would want "mixed bathing." And, while the world goes to Hell with the Church on its heels, nothing— but *nothing*—can make such "issues" other than inane! The world, of course, knows it and so do some in the Church, but the charge sticks.

Friend, the Church is in trouble!!

And the call comes again to us as it did to young Francis of Assisi when he knelt in the forsaken and empty chapel of San Damiano—"RENEW MY CHURCH!"

Step Two on the road to renewal is the affirmation that . . .

THE CHURCH CAN BE SAVED. Jesus' declaration that the gates of death would never prevail against the Church did not include the promise of numbers. It was only a promise that it would not die out. But, He also added, that wherever *two or three* are gathered, it is yet alive! No automatic numerical assurance was ever intended or given us. The numbers require something else!

The Church will survive and can be revived, but never for the purpose of "survival" alone. Those committed to the renewal of the Church must see beyond that! "He who would save his life shall lose it" holds true for the Church as well as the individual. It will survive only as we give it away. Victor Makari, a native Egyptian and Presbyterian minister in Philadelphia, commented that the reason Egyptian Christianity has never been a viable force, though one of the early centers of the Faith, is that for "twenty centuries it has been solely concerned with *survival*"! Our concern must go beyond survival to service!

That it can be saved for service, in spite of the contemporary problems, is indicated by the pockets of "Life" which have begun to emerge in our midst. The wide acceptance of the writings of Keith Miller on renewal, *The Taste of New Wine* and *A Second Touch,* only underscores the widespread hunger which exists in the Christian ranks.[5] Experimental churches, which have provided verifying evidence in a laboratory-like setting, as well as renewed existing churches,

are further indication of the *possibility* of new life in the
Church. Reference is made here to such reports as Eliza-
beth O'Connor's *Call to Commitment*, Ralph Neighbour's
The Seven Last Words of the Church and Wallace Fisher's
From Tradition to Mission.[6] But, let none believe that it will
come without both cost and change!

This second step on the road to renewal leads inevitably
to a third step, a step which is almost a side-step. It is to
pause long enough to objectively consider the question . . .

Is THE CHURCH WORTH SAVING? If it is not, then to talk of
renewal is obviously absurd. It is a question which must be
faced simply because so many committed Christians who
are making telling marks for Christ have abandoned the
Church! These are the ones who are seeking to bear their
witness outside the institutional church and who are not to
be confused with those who go out "from us" because they
are not "of us" in the first place.

It is obvious that some of the most exciting ministries
among the forgotten segments of the outcast world—the
hippies, the drug addicts, the youth, etc.—are being done
outside the institutional church! And what does this say? It
says to some that the institutional church should be jettisoned
if one wants to be where "the action is." The assumption
here is that the Church *cannot* do much, if anything, simply
because it *has not* done much. This is not true!

For those committed to renewal, the option of a churchless world is no option at all. There is far too much to aban-
don in terms of potential and resources within the Church.
The Church, we say, is not bad; it is good. *But, it is not good
enough!*

Step Four is a careful step. We must not miss it. It says
that . . .

CHURCH RENEWAL CANNOT BE DIVORCED FROM PERSONAL
RENEWAL! There is a diabolical joke being pulled on contemporary Christianity which says that it can be! But it
cannot! Renewal begins with *renewed persons!* W. O. Vaught

has well observed that "we cannot go farther until we go deeper." Let no one believe otherwise! *The* problem with the Church does not have to do with structures, organizations, bureaucracy, or ineptness; it has to do with *persons*—you and me!

If new life is to be infused into the Church, it will not come from any impersonal quarter; it will come from *persons*. And therein lies the *price of renewal*. We would do well to re-state Jesus' warning at this point: *count the cost* before you begin!

Finally, Step Five. It is another "awareness" step. It simply says . . .

TIME IS SHORT! Already fifty-eight percent of the college students (a recent poll) say "institutional Christianity is irrelevant." Spiritual statisticians are unanimous in their prediction that, if we continue to reach people at our present rate, organized Christianity will constitute less than two percent of the world population by the year 2000. Krister Stendahl, Dean of the Harvard Divinity School, and many others are predicting "a remnant church only" by the turn of the century.

The shortness of time is evident in other ways, also. Those within the churches, who constitute the source for renewal, are slowly becoming a "ghetto of indifference." Thomas J. Mullen fearfully reported recently:

On one occasion the author was a visiting minister in a large city and in the process of a sermon used an illustration about the exploitation of the poor by slum landlords. The illustration had to do with the fact that slum property, especially in large metropolitan areas, is usually not owned by evil and greasy men who have a working relationship with the Mafia or who sit in plush offices someplace, rubbing their hands together greedily at the very thought of next month's rent. Instead, it was pointed out, slum property is often owned by large, respectable businesses, such as insurance companies, or by friendly, amiable WASPS who simply do not see the connection between their church lives and their business lives.

Immediately after the sermon the resident pastor told me that I had, unknowingly and accidentally, described one member of his congregation almost perfectly. He said that this particular man could not have been more perfectly identified if he had been asked to stand and wave to the congregation. About that time I looked up to see this very man walking toward me, which presented the possibility that we were about to have a genuine confrontation between prophet and sinner.

The confrontation never took place. Instead of anger or remorse or defensiveness, the man clasped my hand, thanked me for the sermon, and asked me if I would be interested in coming to that church as their full-time pastor, since the present minister was leaving soon. My "prophetic" sermon had made *no* impact on that man, at least any that could be observed. I might as well have said nothing. Afterward, the resident pastor and I discussed this event and tried to analyze how such seeming indifference could be possible.[7]

The Church is slowly losing its ears to hear and its eyes to see!

The time is short . . . and shortening! We must move *now!* If not, then, when the death knell rings—

> *Ask not for whom the bell tolls—*
> *It tolls . . . for thee!*

Our basic assumption, then, reads:

> The Church Is in Trouble!
> It Can Be Saved!
> It Is Worth Saving!
> It Must Begin With Me!
> But, Time Is Short!

With these in hand, we must commit ourselves to *renewal!* Thomas Mullen is our encouraging friend when he says: "There is work to be done. It is high time we get at it, for it is our Father's business we are now neglecting."[8]

STUDY HELPS

Chapter One

A. SMALL GROUP CREATIVE PROCEDURE

In Chapter 1, Dr. Haney has suggested the solution to renewing the Church must be a *personal* one. To develop awareness of what he means, create a microcosm of the church within your group. Appoint one of the group as "moderator" and conduct a church "business session" to discuss a motion that the church begin a ministry of some sort (a coffee house or recreation or rehabilitation) to teenagers who are on drugs and who may be runaways. Assign the following "attitudes" to be taken by members of the group. Make the assignments privately or write each on a slip of paper.

1. "I can't stand these kids in the drug culture."
2. "What's wrong with our present programs?"
3. "We've never done anything like this before, never needed to, so why do it now?"
4. "Our building will be ruined."
5. "The time is short."
6. "What will happen if they mix with our children?"
7. "The kids need our help!"
8. "Christ loves those kids; so should we."
9. "We must innovate—or die!"
10. "I'm tired of 'playing religion'."

Continue the discussion until you have earnestly attempted to develop unanimity among the participants. Then evaluate what you have learned, the reasons you are at an impasse, and what further can be done to solve the problem.

B. FOR FURTHER READING

Understanding the Need:
Carlyle Marney. *Structures of Prejudice.* (Nashville: Abingdon, 1961).
Colin Morris. *Include Me Out.* (Nashville: Abingdon, 1968).

Thomas J. Mullen. *Ghetto of Indifference*. (Nashville: Abingdon, 1966).

Alvin Toffler. *Future Shock*. (New York: Random House, 1970). This book is suggested as a study of the societal changes surrounding the Church. While secular in orientation, it is extremely helpful.

Renewal Concepts:

Russell Bow. *The Integrity of Church Membership*. (Waco: Word, 1968).

Findley B. Edge. *A Quest for Vitality in Religion*. (Nashville: Broadman).

Keith Miller. *The Taste of New Wine*. (Waco: Word, 1965). This book is a classic in its own time.

————. *A Second Touch*. (Waco: Word, 1967).

Bob Patterson. *The Stirring Giant*. (Waco: Word, 1971).

Larry Richards. *A New Face for the Church*. (Grand Rapids: Zondervan, 1970).

Elton Trueblood. *Company of the Committed*. (New York: Harper & Row, 1961). This book is considered the classic on renewal.

————. *The Incendiary Fellowship*. (New York: Harper & Row, 1967).

Chapter Two

A UNIVERSAL MINISTRY

Almost all astute observers agree that the growth of the lay or universal ministry is the growing edge of vital Christianity today.

Once we have been captivated by the concept and possibility of a renewed Church in our time, given the basic assumption of its necessity and potential reality, our first question is . . .

How Will a Renewed Church Come Into Being? Where is the pivotal point of turning? Those at the headwaters and in the mainstream of the renewal movement are in unanimous agreement that the hope for renewal lies in *the liberation of the laity.* Call it what you will—the lay ministry, the universal ministry, the equipping ministry—it all means the same: *that every believer is called to be a minister.* Not a "clergyman," mind you—a "minister." John R. Mott first introduced the concept in the 1920's, but somehow it was lost in the shuffle. It was an idea born too soon. But in the 1960's, after lying forgotten in the Temple for a generation, it was "an idea whose time had come" and, as

Victor Hugo taught us, such an idea cannot be stopped by anything. Simultaneously, in 1960-61, without any comparison of notes, three to-be leaders of renewal published books on the theme of renewal *via* the lay ministry: Robert Raines (*New Life in the Church*), Francis O. Ayres (*The Ministry of the Laity*), and Elton Trueblood (*Company of the Committed*).[1]

This concept of an all-inclusive ministry is both *basic* and *biblical*. It is basic to renewal in that every-believer-involvement is both the starting and finish line. Renewal will begin when the lay ministry begins, and its goal is "every believer a minister." It is *biblical* in that it was precisely the point which the Apostle Paul sought to make to the congregation at Ephesus. Said he:

> "And these were his gifts: some to be . . . pastors and teachers, to equip God's people for work in her service."
> (4:11-12 NEB)

Note carefully the last phrase. It is sometimes rendered "for the work of the ministry" (KJV and RSV) or "for the work of ministering" (The Emphasized N.T.). It is the Greek word *diakonias* which is variously translated "minister," "serve," and "work." But the importance of the verse is that it stresses that the function of the pastoral ministry is to equip the believers "for the work of the ministry"!

Not only is it basic and biblical, it is also *Protestant* and *practical*. The heart of the Protestant Reformation is to be found in "the priesthood of the believer." Our understanding of the concept, however, has been somewhat one-sided. We readily see and agree that each is to be his own priest. What is not so readily seen, but which is also implicit, is that each can be a priest to his neighbor! Everyone is a priest! On the *practical* side, the mere numbers involved ought to say something to us. If ministering in the name of Christ is restricted to the professional clergy only, then the vast majority of Christians are excluded. If, however, *all* believers are ministers, then the situation is vastly and numerically altered. As Trueblood has noted:

> We may agree that a professionalized ministry is necessary but not sufficient. The chief reason that it is not sufficient is that the job to be done is *too big to be done by the work of a minority*, no matter how gifted and trained that minority may be. (italics added)[2]

Agreed! And, having agreed, the next question is . . .

How Can the Lay Ministry Be Effected? How are the vast forces of the laity to be liberated, and how may they be included in the ministry of Christ to others? To answer, we turn to some basic definitions.

The Definition of "Ministry." As mentioned above, the word *minister* means "to serve" or "to work." The Greek word is transliterated as "deacon," and the Latin word means "to attend" or "to serve." In the Christian sense of the word, it involves serving others in the name of Christ. Jesus said of Himself, "The Son of Man is not come to be ministered unto, but to minister." One only needs to spend a few moments with a concordance of the Bible to know that "ministry" is that for which the Church exists. Francis O. Ayres has said:

> The point is that the church does not first exist and then decide whether or how it will serve. *The Church exists to serve the world* and has no being except as it is a servant.[3]

No one is excused or exempted from ministry who bears the name of Christ. *No one!*

The Definition of "Pastoral Ministry." If all are ministers, then what is the place and function of the pastor? Whenever one compares the modern conception of what a pastor is to be and to do—in the light of the New Testament—a vast difference is immediately evident! Frankly, most of the modern concept came out of the rural culture of generations past, not the New Testament!

Robert Raines has written succinctly on the pastoral ministry and states:

> The clergyman's abiding frustration is that in doing the many things that are useful, he may be prevented from doing the one thing needful. It is being suggested here that the one thing needful in the role of the clergyman for our time is that he prepare his people for their ministry in the church and in the world. *The chief task of the clergyman is to equip his people for their ministry.* All his work is to this end. The functions of preacher, prophet, pastor, priest, evangelist, counselor, and administrator find their proper places in the equipping ministry. The purpose of this ministry is that the people shall be trained and outfitted for their work in the church and in the world.[4]

One has likened the pastor's role to that of "the playing coach." That is, he does not play *for* them; he teaches *them* how to play and then *joins* them on the field.

Thomas J. Mullen has written on the concept of the equipping ministry with as much insight as any. He views the *equipping minister* as "the builder of community," or the one who draws the people together; "the catalytic agent," or the one who brings together and excites joint labors; "the teacher," or the one who provides the necessary training; and, "the man of truth," the one who lives it out before and with them.[5]

No clearer direction has been given than that of Dr. Trueblood when he wrote:

> The old-fashioned idea was that the pastor had a program, and that the members were his helpers in putting his program into effect. Thus, it has long been understood that lay members have a function, but it has often been seen as little more than an auxiliary function. Women, it has been thought, could be very useful in preparing church suppers or in working with the altar guild, while men could look after the repairs of the building, take up the offering, guide the work of the janitor, and help in the every-member canvass. But the main show was the pastor's; he was the entrepreneur: the Church was his business; and if he were not careful he would refer to the Church as his.

Now, with the new emphasis on what the Church might be in the world, the familiar picture is entirely reversed. At last we are beginning to see that it is the ordinary member who has a program and that the pastor is *his* helper.[6]

The Definition of "Lay Ministry." While we have not yet fully defined the lay ministry, it is obvious that it has nothing to do with "chores about the church"! So many of us are like the pastor who, when asked what he would do if forty or fifty men approached him after a service requesting something to do, replied: "I don't know what it could be; we already have sixty ushers!" Whatever it is, it is not that!

The lay ministry involves a "call." Paul urged the Ephesian members to "walk worthy of your vocation"; not the *pastor*, but the *members*. And, the word "vocation" comes from the Latin *vocatio* meaning "to call"! We each have a call. In fact, *two* calls. One is a General Call. That is, *all* believers are called to be those "in whom Christ is felt to live again." The other is a Specific Call—to a unique and personal ministry within the Kingdom of God. It could entail lay speaking, distributing Christian literature, visiting, administration, encouragement, teaching a class in Sunday school, aiding an indigent ministry, and on and on. But we each have a specific ministry to which Christ calls us. The various lists of gifts in the New Testament include many tasks that could never be construed to have reference to the professional clergy; they are "gifts" and "calls" for the laity! (See I Corinthians 12:28; Ephesians 4:11-12).

The concept of the Universal Ministry is the most exciting discovery in the twentieth century expression of Christianity! Yet, in a sense, it is not a discovery; it is a *recovery* . . . of authentic, New Testament Christianity. In light of it, can you—even for just a moment—imagine. . .

WHAT A RENEWED CHURCH WOULD BE LIKE? Putting it all together, can you envision a church in which the *sole* function of the pastor is to *equip* the people for their ministries? See him as he forsakes his mimeograph and budgeting (leav-

ing it to those whose ministry it is) and teaches and organizes
task groups and study groups, as he preaches, as he visits
(with a layman to teach him how), and as he prays and
studies to be a better equipper? Can you visualize a membership who considered themselves as *all* being a part of the
working crew with no passenger list? Each is seeking his
ministry and many have found it. They turn to the pastor to
enlist his help in sharpening their skills for *their* ministries.
Groups are clustered here and there around tasks and func-
tions and ministries. Some are in the ghetto, some among the
hippies, others among the doctors and the lawyers. Some are
involved in physical and economic assistance, others are in
direct spiritual ministries—but all of the tasks are infused
with the Christ-message. *Can you imagine?*

But has it ever been so? We need look no further than the
New Testament for verification! The book of Acts, the earliest report of the Church's activity, is evidence *par excellence.* "Every member involvement" was far more than a
mere slogan to them; it was their strategy! Notice how, in
the book of Acts, before the laity really became involved,
that the term for converts was "added"—the Lord "added"
to the Church. But when the *people (laos)* were scattered
abroad, when they could not be apostle-centered and when
they had to spread the Word (or else!)—the term became
"multiplied"! This is underscored in the act of adding dea-
cons to the Church structure in Acts 6. Immediately following their selection and induction is the statement: "and the
word of God increased, and the number of the disciples was
multiplied" (Acts 6:7). Therein is the "secret"! The liberation of the laity; indeed, the abolition of the laity! *All in the
ministry!!*

How? How? How? It is obvious that if it is to come in
our time, several things must be clearly underscored and
grasped. *First,* the "balcony view" concept of the laity is *out!*
We must view it from the stage itself where *we* are the
actors and only *One* constitutes the Audience.

Second, change of any kind, but especially in the Church,
does not come without cost. The old and time-honored (and

less-than-effective) division of labor—Clergy and Laity—is deeply entrenched and, quite frankly, *enjoyed.* It is enjoyed by lay men and women who prefer paying another to do their religion for them. A weekly audience and a dollar contribution is a cheap and easy "out"—and a pretty good bargain! But, whatever else the Christian life is, it is not something that *anyone* can do *for* another! On the other hand, it is *enjoyed* by many pastors. They enjoy the counterfeit status it gives them ("the *Reverend* Mr. Jones") and view with alarm the idea that all are "ministers." The very idea! They both view the liberation of the laity as an extremely dangerous idea. *And it is!*

Third, it is obvious that if the lay forces are to be brought out of reserve and put into the fight, then the troops must be trained. The following chapters, then, will deal with the *equipment* and the *equipping* of the saints for the work of the ministry.

Paul's instruction to Archippus is our mandate, too: "See that you fulfill the ministry which you have received of the Lord" (Colossians 4:17).

STUDY HELPS

Chapter Two

A. SMALL GROUP CREATIVE PROCEDURE

Your group should imagine itself to be an initial body of Christians who have gathered themselves together to organize a new congregation. *Your only resources are yourselves.* All ministries must be conducted, utilizing only the spiritual gifts within your fellowship. Your geographical location is in the very heart of 15,000 apartments, among families with a middle-class income. In the time available, determine what strategy you would utilize to:

1. Worship
2. Conduct Bible Study for all ages
3. Witness
4. Equip yourselves for ministry
5. ' Create family-oriented spiritual growth
6. Insure a deep level of fellowship within the congregation
7. Select a pastor

When you have finished, poll each person in the group for a frank appraisal as to their willingness to belong to such a congregation in real life, *and why.*

With this appraisal in mind, discuss the possibilities of it in an existing congregation. What steps would be required to move toward the goals? What different transitional steps would be required?

Finally, apply this approach to (a) a new congregation in *your city* and (b) to the transitional steps in your own congregation.

B. For Further Reading

The Equipping Ministry:

Thomas J. Mullen. *The Renewal of the Ministry.* (Nashville: Abingdon, 1963). This book is one of a kind on the pastoral ministry. Very good.

Robert Raines. *New Life in the Church.* (New York: Harper & Row, 1961).

The Universal Ministry:

Francis O. Ayres. *The Ministry of the Laity.* (Philadelphia: Westminster, 1962).

Kenneth Chafin. *Help I'm a Layman.* (Waco: Word, 1966).

Elton Trueblood. *Alternative to Futility.* (New York: Harper & Row, 1948).

————. *The Yoke of Christ.* (New York: Harper & Row, 1958).

————. *Your Other Vocation.* (New York: Harper & Row, 1952).

Chapter Three

A BELIEVING STANCE

*We are now in a kind of intellectual vacuum in which somebody could fill the space if he would. It would probably have to be a group, a group who are strongly rational at the same time they are deeply committed and unapologetic in their Christian commitment.**

If the lay ministry is to achieve its fullest potential in terms of an effective witness—in *our* world—the lay minister must be theologically competent and articulate. Far too much attention in our pragmatic age has been given to what the Church and the Christian stand *for* and/or *against* without the prior consideration of what we stand *on*. For it is what one *believes* which ultimately determines what he will *do*.

Equally so, there is a negative incentive for doctrinal awareness. The Faith is under attack in our day simply because it is *faith*. Science, with its emphasis on objectivity and verification, has made us all skeptical of anything which

*From an interview with Dr. Elton Trueblood. Quoted from *Christianity Today* by permission.

smacks of "experience" and "faith." Many, who have known no other educational and environmental milieu, have simply ruled out—*a priori*—any such consideration. One who would bear witness today had best know whereof he speaks! It is true that there has never been a time when there was not a need for the ability to give "a reason for the hope that is in us," but it is also true that there has never been a time when it was more necessary.

One of the problems which the renewing church must face is that, in large measure, the beliefs we hold are not our own! Our present doctrinal legacy is, for the most part, from the Protestant Reformation to the early part of this century. Its only force now is that of momentum. Most of it was written to negate and, consequently, is couched in rather dogmatic terms. Ours, however, is an age which demands the positive and the affirmative. And since our beliefs are really not our own, they have the tendency to be cliché-ridden and trite. (Not long ago a committed young lady commented on a guest speaker's message by assessing, "What he said was true, but it was the same old clichés!") A par-roted faith simply will not suffice.

This is not to say that all, or any part, of our doctrinal legacy is or was untrue! Rather, it is to say that a Faith, if it is to be a vital force for living, must be matched over against the needs, the problems and the fears *of the day*. One theologian has commented that for generations past the great need which faith met was *guilt*; now, however, the need is *meaning*. Whether this is true in whole or in part, it does point up the need for a relevant faith *vis-a-vis* the contemporary needs. It is also to say that our beliefs must be *our* beliefs. It is like the sign in the bookstore window: "Second Hand Theology For Sale." We need a *first edition!*

WHY—A BASIC FAITH?[1] Suffice it to say that it is not to have a storehouse of information. The Apostle Paul warned about "ever learning, but never coming to the truth"! (II Timothy 3:7). Far too many of us have become modern-day Athenians who spend their time "in nothing else, but either to tell, or to hear, some new thing" (Acts 17:21).

Among those who seek renewal, a basic faith is needed for at least three primary reasons: First, there is a *personal* need. That is, one needs a basic faith simply because it will determine how he lives, where he stands, and what he does. In all the variations which life affords, a basic faith becomes both a place to stand and a base from which to operate.

Second, there is a *witnessing* need. When one is called upon, or seeks to be called upon, for a witness *today*—he must be able to produce the \goods! While there are still pockets of people around who do not require a reasoned faith, they are a decreasing minority. And where these pockets have disappeared a new breed exists who will not be swayed by a simple "word of testimony."

Third, there is a *recovering* need. In the more academically and technologically oriented cosmopolitan centers, there is to be found an increasing number of persons who stand somewhere between the "saved" and "lost" designations: *the spiritual drop-outs*. These are persons with a rich religious heritage, an early life of commitment in the Church, but whose faith has been subverted somewhere along the way. Because a cliché-ridden, second-hand theology met a sophisticated unbelieving professor, or because an inadequate and indefensible superstitious faith met obvious truth in science and philosophy (or whatever)—they lost faith—and dropped out! Turned off by dogmatic assertions, which they knew could not be verified, they turned away. And, in many ways, their recovery holds the promise of the future.

A faith which is a *faith* will accomplish *at least* these three things. But, the next question immediately asks . . .

WHAT—A BASIC FAITH? The key to a basic faith is the word "basic." Dr. Robert Naylor has drawn the helpful distinction between opinion and conviction: an "opinion" is something *you hold*; a "conviction" is something that *holds you*. A basic faith has to do with *convictions*, not *opinions*. It is far more than an idle exercise to think through and write out one's own personal theology or creed and, even more important, to afterward assess what constitutes opinion and what constitutes conviction. *You have no basic faith apart from such an exercise!* Anything else is a parroted, second-hand variety—no matter how good or how true it may be! If one is to have a *basic* faith, somewhere along the way (indeed, all along the way) it must be personally developed.

Why not now?

Why not—right now—write out your own personal theology? What do *you*, not your denomination, your church, your pastor, but *you*—what do you believe about:

God, the Trinity: _____

_____

_____

_____

_____

Jesus Christ: _____

_____

_____

_____

_____

The Holy Spirit: _____

_____

_____

_____

_____

The Scriptures: _____

_____

_____

_____

_____

The Church of Jesus Christ: _____

_____

_____

_____

_____

Salvation—Its Need and Means: _____

_____

_____

_____

_____

Baptism: _____

_____

_____

_____

_____

The Lord's Supper: _____

_____

_____

_____

_____

The Life Everlasting: _____

_____

_____

_____

_____

Stewardship: _____

_____

_____

_____

_____

Witnessing: _____

_____

_____

_____

_____

After having written your personal theology, differentiate between the opinions and the convictions in it. To illustrate more forcefully, some time ago—as a result of a chain of events and reading—I decided to *honestly* preach a sermon on "Beliefs for Which I Would Die." Knowing of the Apostle Paul and Stephen in the New Testament, post-biblical martyrs like Polycarp and Felix Manz, and modern ones like Bill Wallace and Jim Elliott, I tried to honestly locate those beliefs for which *I* was willing to die. I found, quite candidly, that I believed many good and churchly things for which . . . I *would not* die! But, there were *some* things that I felt I would be obligated to hold at any cost. What mine are is of no consequence to you. What are *you* willing to die for?[2]

One helpful note, however, before you begin such an exciting endeavor is the reminder of where the early disciples began. While they had a backlog of Old Testament information (no one knows how much), their faith-walk began with their encounter with Jesus of Nazareth. They met Him, He called them, they followed, and He changed their lives. *Their theology was an attempt to explain what they had experienced.* And that is what real theology is!

Thus, the earliest known creed was simply, "Jesus is Lord." This is the accurate Greek translation of Romans 10:9 which, usually rendered "confess with thy mouth the Lord Jesus," literally means: "That if thou shalt confess 'Jesus is Lord' . . . thou shalt be saved." Begin there—*Jesus is Lord!* Theology does not begin with "God"; Jesus is the One who revealed to us most of what we know about God! Theology does not begin with the "New Testament"; there were disciples (Christians) before there was a New Testament! While the New Testament is our basic source about Jesus Christ, it is not the beginning place of our theology: it tells us about *Him.* Starting, then, with Christ—with the full belief that He is the one absolute Source and Center of our faith—ask: *What did Jesus believe?* This may (or may not) cause some revisions in our beliefs, but it is the only proper place for *Christians* to begin.[3]

Therein lies the answer to "What—a Basic Faith?" The next step is just as obvious as the former . . .

HOW—A BASIC FAITH? The value of what others have said and written on *the* Faith is that of testing and refining *our* Faith. What others have believed and how they have tested and refined each other's beliefs across these two thousand years of Christian history *is not to be discounted*, especially if we believe in the timeless ability of the Holy Spirit to enlighten and to guide! They are your allies—use them!

The local church to which you belong is your most immediate ally. Through its regular educational programs, much is made available to you. The church can also provide special series in doctrine and theology. Retreats can be sponsored by the local church with a doctrinal theme. The pastor can preach and teach on the why, the what, and the how of belief. Use your church!

Your denomination also provides an ally for you in your quest for a personal faith. Most denominations offer summer assemblies, organized classes in seminaries and seminary extension centers, and local and regional conferences. Many even offer home study correspondence courses. Ask and you shall receive! Use your denomination!

Inter-denominational efforts are also a possibility. Many local ministerial groups offer lay academies and special seminars which can be of value. While it is true that one may encounter beliefs with which he cannot agree, it is also true that we often find more in common than we ever realized possible. Every denominational seminary finds students from other denominations attending with little difficulty and much value. While such a pursuit should be first investigated (ask your pastor!), it may be just the ally you need.

But—no organized group study, no matter how good, can ever take the place of *personal* and *disciplined* study! One who would be competent is one who must study on his own. But, what? and how? While the "how" is the subject of a subsequent chapter, some suggestions on the "what" of study can be made here.

The Bible is, of course, primary in your study. To aid your study, secure a good Bible dictionary, a theological "word book," and a one-volume Bible commentary.[4] Later on, a more detailed multi-volume commentary can be added. A good place to begin is with the history in the Bible, i.e., how the events developed: Old Testament history, the life of Jesus, the life of Paul, etc. After that, one can study individual books of the Bible or themes within the Bible, such as redemption, the Holy Spirit, or witnessing.

Theology is another needed area of study. The place to begin is with your denominational beliefs. Expand it, then, to read the great theologians of history: Augustine, Luther, Calvin, and some of the more recent theologians. The method which has proved most helpful is to begin with a systematic study of beliefs and then proceed to specific theologians.

Philosophy is yet another discipline of benefit, especially the philosophy of religion. As one seeks to bear witness in *our* age, no "arsenal" is complete without sound thinking practices. One student who had jettisoned the Bible as authoritative in any sense asked me, "Is there a case for God apart from the Bible?" When one will not accept the Bible as the common ground, whether he is an atheist or a Moslem, other means are necessary.

Many other areas are available, as well: ethics, Christian history, biblical languages and the like. This, or something comparable, is required if we are to have *a believing stance.*

Carlyle Marney put his finger on it when he wrote:

> The aim of the church is not to enlist its laymen into the services of the church—our aim is to put laymen as theological competents in the service of the world.[5]

STUDY HELPS

Chapter Three

A. SMALL GROUP CREATIVE PROCEDURE

Begin with a discussion of the meaning of Dr. Haney's assertions regarding our faith not being our own, but a parroted faith. Each member of the group should next be asked to spend approximately thirty minutes in silence, recording in one or two sentences the statement of personal theology (see pages 40-41). Taking one theological statement at a time, let each person read aloud what has been written. Allow time for discussion of differences and seek to understand why they exist.

Next, discuss the group's doctrinal statements in light of the idea of "conviction" and "opinion," employing the standard of "beliefs for which to die."

Conclude with group discussion as to what further might be required before the members would feel adequate in having "a faith to share."

B. FOR FURTHER READING

Myron Augsburger. *Faith for a Secular Age World.* (Waco: Word, 1968).

Emil Brunner. *Our Faith.* (New York: Scribners, 1960).

W. T. Conner. *Christian Doctrine.* (Nashville: Broadman, 1937).

Carl F. H. Henry, ed. *Basic Christian Doctrines.* (New York: Holt, Rinehart, 1962).

C. S. Lewis. *Mere Christianity.* (New York: Macmillan, 1943).

Elton Trueblood. *A Place to Stand.* (New York: Harper & Row, 1969).

J. S. Whale. *Christian Doctrine.* (London: Cambridge University Press, 1961).

Chapter Four

A DISCIPLINED WALK

*The price of excellence is discipline
and the continuance of discipline.*

That Jesus called His first followers "disciples" cannot be
argued. Just a cursory examination of the gospels is the only
verification required. And, the fact that this was *His* choice
of words is important: it indicates how *He* viewed His followers. The definition has to do with teaching, learning, and
following instructions. From the word "disciple" comes the
word "discipline." It was all this which Jesus had in mind
when He said His followers were to be known as "disciples."

Disciplined—by Whom? Christian discipline is as much
an *attitude* as it is an *activity*: the attitude of submission to
another in order to learn. For the disciples of Christ it is
obvious that the "another" is *Jesus Christ*.

There is a sense in which Christian discipline is self-
discipline, for it cannot exist without consent and a willingness to respond. However, Christ is the initiator: He directs
and the Christian responds. It is self under the control of
Christ: *disposably His.* Perhaps the best synonym available
to us is "meekness." The Greek word *praos* (meek) was

used to describe the war horses of the ancient armies! Meek? Yes! For it meant that all of their strength and power was under the absolute control of the rider. It did not remove the strength; it controlled it. And that is Christian discipleship.

DISCIPLINED—IN WHAT? The most common error in understanding the concept of Christian discipleship is that of limiting it to specific areas when it is *total* and all-encompassing. Discipline refers to life itself: a disciplined life.

Three books which have been immensely helpful at the point of discipline's scope are: Kierkegaard's *Purity of Heart Is to Will One Thing*, Thomas Kelly's *A Testament of Devotion*, and Douglas Steere's *On Beginning From Within*. The stress of each of them is that *singularity* is the key to discipline: the Christ-life *must* become, not merely the chief goal of life, but the *only* goal. As Douglas Steere wrote:

> The saint is . . . a man or a woman who has become clear as to exactly what he wants of all there is in the world, and whom a love at the heart of things has so satisfied, that he *gaily reduces his cargo to make for that port.* (italics added)[1]

As with Paul, the disciplined Christian must become a "one-thinger" (Philippians 3:13). Jesus was evidently thinking of the same thing when He said, "When thine eye is single thy whole body is full of light" (Luke 11:34). The disciplined Christian is the one who says with the anonymous wise man: "if you would do *this*, you cannot do *that*." The Christ-life has a single focus and it involves "reducing the cargo"—of necessity.

Thus, discipline ultimately has to do with time, for *time* is what *life* is. Everyone of us is equal at the point of time: we are each allotted twenty-four hours a day, no more and no less. But, how we employ that time is something else! If one would be a disciple, he will order that time under the control of Christ. This, and this alone, is the key to an effective life. E. Herman has expressed it thus:

When we read the lives of the saints, we are struck by a certain large leisure which went hand in hand with a remarkable effectiveness. They were never hurried. They did comparatively few things, and these not necessarily striking or important; and they troubled very little about their influence. Yet, they always seemed to hit the mark; every bit of their life *told*. Their simplest actions had a distinction, an exquisiteness which suggested the artist. The reason is not far to seek. Their sainthood lay in their habit of referring the smallest actions to God. They lived in God. They acted from a pure motive of love towards God. They were as free from self-regard as from slavery to the good opinion of others. God's Son and God rewarded; what else needed they? Hence the inalienable dignity of these meek, quiet figures that seem to produce such marvelous effects with such humble materials.[2]

There it is! The secret! There is *no other* way!

While discipline is life-wide, it also has some specific focal points within the life, some of which are more important than others. Our next step is to ask . . .

DISCIPLINED—IN WHAT? In what specific areas is discipline more important? Here we shall deal with two areas: discipline in the *life of devotion* and discipline in the *life of ministry*.

THE LIFE OF DEVOTION

Mark it down as a spiritual axiom that there is no mastery in the Christian life apart from a disciplined devotional life—Bible reading and prayer!

Look first at PRAYER. The fact that Jesus prayed is extremely important. Jesus *prayed*. It is equally important to note that the disciples, so far as we know, never asked Jesus to teach them how to preach or to teach, but . . . "teach us how to *pray*"! Additionally, in understanding the nature of prayer, it is important to see that the emphasis which Jesus gave to prayer was that of *private "closet" praying*. This does not exclude public prayer, such as is offered in corporate worship, but none can escape the fact that the emphasis which Jesus gave to prayer, by example and lesson, was on the *personal* prayer life. Given these crucial guidelines, we can ask of prayer's nature and character.

Prayer is both spoken and meditative. That is, sometimes prayer involves our speaking to God, silently or aloud, and sometimes it is merely waiting before God, quietly and expectantly.

Spoken prayer takes the form of requests, thanksgivings, confessions and appeals. The Pattern Prayer which Jesus gave to us, usually called the Lord's Prayer, majors on requests: Thy will be done, daily bread, forgiveness, and deliverance (Luke 11:1-4). Three critically important facets to spoken prayer are: be personal, be honest, be specific!

Be personal! That is, you have a relationship with God like that of Father and child. Speak to God in personal terms. While "Thee" and "Thou" may have their place in public worship, personal worship and prayer are usually better without them. God knows you; you know Him; access at any time has been granted to you: *be personal!*

Be honest! First, because you cannot hide anything from God anyway! Second, because you need not fear God—you have been *accepted*—as you are—into His family. Therefore, if you have sin in your life, be honest about it. If you are unwilling to give it up, be honest about that. If you are willing for God to make you willing, be honest about that, too. God *knows* you, through and through! To be honest is both a *privilege* and a *possibility* for it gives God a unique opening into your life.

Be specific! One of the handicaps to effective prayer is "generalizing." Be *specific* in your requests, your gratitude, your confessions, and your appeals. Instead of saying, "Bless my family," pray for them by name asking *specific* blessings for them which will meet their needs at the moment. Instead of, "Forgive my sins," be specific about the individual sins— pride, envy, or whatever it may be in your life. Nothing dynamic can happen until it becomes specific!

Meditative prayer, on the other hand, is quietly and sin-

cerely waiting before God to give Him an opportunity to
address Himself to us. This is not apt to result in God speaking aloud, but most likely through "impressions" He makes
upon us. Along this line, E. Stanley Jones advocates ending
spoken prayer with, "And now, God, is there anything You
want to say to me?" and then to wait silently for awhile.
Meditative prayer, also, is to allow the Holy Spirit to call
things to our attention which we should introduce into our
spoken prayers (Romans 8:26-27). Thomas Kelly is our
guide at the point of this deeper dimension of meditative
prayer. He says:

> There come times when prayer pours forth in volumes and
> originality such as we cannot create. It rolls through us like
> a mighty tide. Our prayers are mingled with a vaster Word,
> a Word that at one time was made flesh. We pray, and yet
> it is not we who pray, but a Creator who prays in us. Some-
> thing of our punctiform selfhood is weakened, but never lost.
> All we can say is, Prayer is taking place, and I am given to
> be in the orbit. . . .
>
> Sometimes this prayer is particularized, and we are impelled
> to pray for particular persons or particular situations with
> a quiet or turbulent energy that, subjectively considered,
> seems utterly irresistible. Sometimes the prayer and this Life
> that flows through us reaches out to all souls with kindred
> vision and upholds them in His tender care. Sometimes it
> flows out to the world of blinded struggle, and we become
> cosmic Saviors, seeking all those who are lost.
>
> This "infused prayer" is not frequently given, in full inten-
> sity. But something of its autonomous character remains, not
> merely as a memory of a time when the fountains of creation
> were once revealed and we were swept along in their rising
> waters. It remains as an increasing awareness of a more-
> than-ourselves, working persuadingly and powerfully at the
> roots of our own soul, and in the depths of all men.[3]

The point of discipline in prayer is that of *consistency*. The
greatest hindrance, conversely, is the lack of regularity. Every
believer *must* have a definite time (if not, times) for prayer
each day. The *best* time is first thing in the morning. This

way, you can "pray through the day" ahead of you, anticipating what will happen and praying over your response to it. At night, before retiring, is another good time; it allows one to review the day, to assess failures and their causes, and to rejoice over victories. Above all, do not allow "table grace" and "bedtime" prayers to be the sum total of your prayer life!

Trueblood says: "If you can turn to God, at any time of the day or night, as naturally and unpretentiously as a child turning to his mother, you have found the secret of the saints."[4]

Next, look at BIBLE READING. The Bible does not come to us primarily as a theology textbook with chapters on the doctrine of God, Christ, the Church, etc. Rather, it takes the form of historical account. Yet, it is a special kind of history, i.e., it is the written record of God's acts and activities, in history, with individual men and with groups. This, then, tells us something about the Bible and its purpose: it is to tell us what others have seen and heard and learned of God. It is, therefore, to confirm and encourage our faith (Romans 10:17).

As you read the Bible, then, read it in just that way: I am reading what God has said and done in the past, written by men "inspired" of God (II Timothy 3:16), and it is valuable to me in that it gives me clues as to how the changeless God will act with me and to what He expects from me.

There are two ways in which we read the Bible:

First, we read it in the sense of *study*. That is, we read in order to *learn* from it. One way to do this is through organized group study in such things as Sunday school or Bible Study groups. This way, we add the benefit of a teacher, study helps (such as quarterlies and textbooks), and the reactions of others in the group. It is valuable in that it is *systematic* study—through a book of the Bible or on a theme of the Bible.

Another way of study is that of private, individual study. By accumulating books on the Bible, along with various translations, one can study books and themes privately. Both of these are valuable methods. By applying but fifteen minutes a day one can learn so much.

Dr. James Mahoney advocates a two-fold method of personal Bible study: (1) Condensation and (2) Conduct. That is, Step One in personal Bible study, in an attempt to understand its meaning, is to *condense* the particular passage in your own words. Step Two is to seek for *conduct* principles to apply to your own life. To do this, Dr. Mahoney suggests a battery of questions to ask of the passage. Is there . . . "an example to follow, an error to avoid, a promise to claim, a duty to perform, a prayer to echo, a sin to confess, a truth to learn?" Apart from this method (or one like it), the valuable study will be lost.

To read the Bible another way is to do it in a *meditative* sense. This means to read it, fully expecting the Holy Spirit to again claim the words of the Bible and address them to you, *personally*. It is my custom to preface such devotional reading with the words of the Psalmist: "My heart is ready, O God, my heart is ready" (Psalm 108:1 rsv). By approaching the Scriptures in this manner, the testimony of thousands of believers across the years is that the Spirit of God makes the Word become *your* word for that day or time! Such experiences are precious and of immeasurable value to an effective life in Christ.

Again, the secret is *disciplined regularity.* "Man cannot live by bread alone," Jesus taught us; "but by every word of God" (Luke 4:4).

There are two other helpful aspects to the life of devotion which are often overlooked, but with great loss. Those who have been "discoverers" in the inner life all agree to the immeasurable value of the great devotional classics. To know what others have experienced and known is not a guarantee that it will be duplicated in you, but it does make you aware of the *possibilities*. Classics such as the ones mentioned earlier, Augustine's *Confessions, The Imitation of Christ* by Thomas à Kempis, *The Little Flowers of St. Francis of Assisi,*[5] and such evangelical books as Maxwell's *Born Crucified* and Huegel's *Bone of His Bone*[6] are extremely beneficial.

The other aspect is a natural outgrowth of the former: *your own* spiritual diary. Hardbound journals may be purchased at any drug store which will suffice. One can begin in the front with comments about the preceding day and possibilities for the pending day. These need not be lengthy; perhaps a paragraph or two and it may include a written prayer. Next, one can read his scripture for the day and note it in the journal—the passage read and the *personal* message received from it. Prayer may then follow. The requests can be listed in the journal, also: "Today I prayed for. . . ."

In fact, a separate page, perhaps beginning in the back of the journal, can be used for a "Prayer List." This eliminates the ever-plaguing problem of forgotten prayer requests! The surprise to this method is—*the shortness of time required.* By following such a procedure, one *disciplines* himself and, consequently, gets the job done thoroughly and with dispatch!

Those whose spiritual depth we admire most will singularly point to a disciplined life of devotion.

The second area of discipline to which we look is . . .

THE LIFE OF MINISTRY

If we take seriously the Universal Ministry, that we each are called to a life of ministry, we will also take seriously the need for training. Each of us has the same *general* call to live a life through which Christ can care again. This necessitates the above-mentioned devotional life and the need for the basic skills common to all Christians mentioned in Chapter Three.

Here, however, we have reference to the *specific, particular* ministry to which each is called: teaching, visiting, caring for drug abusers or whatever. If this is our call, it requires all of the refinement available to us. One can cut wood with a dull axe, it is true, but a sharp one is much better . . . and easier! But what does this involve? The answer is as personal as is the call, but these two illustrations might be helpful.

First, the Yokefellow Group of the Heritage Baptist Chuch in Annapolis, Maryland, reached the point where the "sense of the meeting" was that Christ was calling them to a *new way*. For three years the group had "collected." They met monthly, on Saturday nights, and studied the Christ-life. The group grew. It grew until some twenty couples were involved. Then, the "call" came. The unanimous leading was that the group was to break up into smaller "clusters" for different ministries: Bible studies, action groups, sharing groups, etc. However, rather than to rush immediately into it, they held a one-day "crash" retreat to study small group dynamics and to study the various possibilities of small group activity. A sharpened axe!

Second, a Sunday school teacher of young couples found herself being constantly called upon for counseling in family and marital problems. She saw it as an opening door of ministry, but recognized a need for training. After a great deal of investigation, she located a course in "Family Therapy" at a nearby state hospital. She enrolled and studied at some expense in time and money. But, a sharpened axe!

If one would minister, let him discipline his ministry!

The life of devotion and the life of ministry are the two definite *foci* of discipline. The hours invested in disciplined preparation are not lost—ever. The truth is, they make the hours spent in ministry doubly productive!

STUDY HELPS

Chapter Four

A. SMALL GROUP CREATIVE PROCEDURE

Using the following format as a "model," let the group shape a Discipline it feels should be required of all members in the future.

Model

1. I will spend a minimum of thirty minutes daily in prayer and scripture reading.
2. I will faithfully attend weekly worship.
3. I will actively participate in a group which serves in ministering to others.
4. I will give a minimum of a tithe of my income to the church.
5. I will make a consistent effort to meet everyone through the day in a spirit of love.
6. I will involve myself in a personal, continuing relationship with unbelievers, including a verbal witness.

_____

(Name)

If the "model" is revised downward, examine the motives behind doing so. When you have finished your structure of the discipline, ask each group member to issue a frank statement as to his or her willingness to abide by it, explaining fully his or her statement.

B. FOR FURTHER READING

E. M. Bounds. *Power Through Prayer*. (Grand Rapids: Zondervan, 1962).

W. M. Clow. *The Secret of the Lord*. (Grand Rapids: Baker, 1955).

Thomas R. Kelly. *A Testament of Devotion*. (New York: Harper & Row, 1941).

Soren Kierkegaard. *Purity of Heart*. (New York: Harper Torchbooks, 1948).

Keith Miller. *Habitation of Dragons*. (Waco: Word, 1970).

Rosalind Rinker. *Prayer—Conversing With God*. (Grand Rapids: Zondervan, 1959).

Douglas Steere. *On Beginning From Within*. (New York: Harper & Row, 1964).

Elton Trueblood. *The New Man for Our Time*. (New York: Harper & Row, 1970).

Chapter Five

A WITNESSING LIFE

The nonwitnessing follower of Christ is a contradiction in terms.

That we are called to a life of witness is evident in that Christ's first word of command was a directive to witness ("Let your light so shine before men . . .") as were His last recorded words on earth ("Ye shall be witnesses . . ."). Elton Trueblood has observed:

Any careful reader of the Gospels is bound to be struck by the obvious effort of Christ to make His hearers understand the nature of His cause. The effort was marked by the tireless use of a great many figures. He told His little company that they were the *salt* of the earth, that they were the *light* of the world, that He had turned over the *keys* of the kingdom; He compared His own work to that of *bread* and of *water*; He said the kingdom was like *leaven*; He said He had come to cast *fire* on the earth. At first the variety of these figures is bewildering, but a powerful insight comes when we realize, suddenly, what they have in common. Each figure represents some kind of penetration. The purpose of the salt is to penetrate the meat and thus preserve it; the function of light is to penetrate the darkness; the only use of the keys is to penetrate the lock; bread is worthless until it penetrates the body; water penetrates the hard crust of earth; leaven penetrates the dough, to make it rise; fire continues only as it reaches new fuel, and the best way to extinguish it is to contain it.

The cumulative effect of all of these figures is almost overwhelming. In any case, they make absolutely clear what the function of Christ's company is meant to be.[1]

The Church exists to *penetrate!* Apart from it we have no reason to exist!

Yet, the cumulated stereotypes of witnessing are sufficient to frighten and/or repulse most would-be witnesses into silence. It is the picture of a person with a Bible as big as a catalog under his arm knocking on doors. It is the picture of a person passing out tracts on a busy street corner. It is the picture of one person "button-holing" another person with a barrage of scripture passages. And, many a would-be witness says—include me out!

Urie Bender lists a number of things which *are not* witnessing. He says:

> Although witness may be an element in any one of these, witnessing is not defined precisely as:
> 1. Ringing doorbells in a community survey.
> 2. Handing out pieces of literature.
> 3. Asking an individual if he is born again.
> 4. Quoting the customary soul-winning passages.
> 5. Preaching a brief sermon filled with moralistic advice.
> 6. Asking for a response of commitment.
> 7. Getting a person to his knees.
> I repeat. In the strictest sense of the word, from the viewpoint of both the dictionary and the Scriptures, witness is none of these.[2]

WHAT WITNESSING IS. Whatever else witnessing involves, it begins with the first person singular out of the context of personal experience. The Apostle John gave us a clue to its nature when he wrote, "That which we have seen and heard, declare we unto you" (I John 1:3). Witnessing involves one sharing out of his own experience. As Bender says, "To witness is to share. Haltingly, perhaps. Without polish, usually. Out of experience, always."[3]

The *content* of the witness has to do with Christ and His workings in the human life. We bear witness . . . *of Him.* By word of mouth and way of life, the believer points beyond himself to One who has wrought the miracle of a new Center in his or her life.

As anyone may ascertain from reading, the book of Acts indicates this to be the method of the earliest Christians. They had no denomination to promote, no program to sell, no tracts to distribute, no building to which they could invite, and no New Testament upon which to rely for their "approach"! Just an experience . . . and . . . a word of witness! It was intensely personal . . . one-to-one . . . and it came with an unmistakable sense of urgency. The Apostle Paul is a case in point. Three times in Acts Paul's personal "testimony" is given. One is the record of it in a biographical account. The other two, however, are reports of Paul giving it to others. This, at least, indicates it was Paul's primary method: *personal witness out of experience.*

Valid witnessing involves two basic elements which, though they can be supplemented, cannot be replaced. They are the *terminus ad quem* of witnessing:

A Way of Life. If our witness is pointed beyond ourselves to the One who has wrought a change within us, then our lives constitute the only verifying data available. What, then, constitutes the "Christian way of life"? Sadly, for most, it constitutes external positives or negatives. Negatively, for some, living the Christ-life is defined in terms of what one does not do: smoke, drink, dance, attend movies, or curse. Positively, for others, it involves what one does: prays, reads the Bible, attends church, and pays his bills. The testimony of one such person is as follows:

> I used to go every Sunday to the priest's house to learn how to be a good Christian. When we did well, we got sweets and tea to take home. Once I got a prize for learning the Four Gospels by heart and reciting them non-stop in the Church.

Who? *Nikita Khrushchev!*

While the Christ-way of necessity involves new and better activities, the verifying factor is a *new Center*, not new externals. It is a life singularly focused on Him. It is a life in which Christ is felt to live again and through which He can again care. It is a life of caring concern and concerned caring; of a wholesome winsomeness and a winsome wholesomeness. The truth is—it is the life which verifies or denies that new Center. Both hypocrisy and super-piety are inevitably counter-productive. The world longs to see that wholeness, that authentic life-reality which Christ alone can give.

A Word of Mouth. Witnessing, must go beyond the *Life* to a verbal explanation of it if it is to be effective. The "word" must "become flesh," it is true, but it is first and last *a word*. For one to say, in effect, that "I let my life speak" borders on a level of pride most unbecoming of a Christian. Trueblood says:

> The spoken word is never really effective unless it is backed up by a life, but it is also true that the living deed is never adequate without the support which the spoken word can provide. This is because no life is ever good enough. The person who says naively, "I don't need to preach; I just let my life speak," is insufferably self-righteous. What one among us is so good that he can let his life speak and leave it at that?

> There has to be a verbal witness because there cannot be communication of important *convictions* without language. "I cannot by being good," says Samuel M. Shoemaker, "tell of Jesus' atoning death and resurrection, nor of my faith in His divinity. The emphasis is too much on me, and too little on Him." We must use words because our faith must be in something vastly greater than ourselves. We make a witness by telling not *who* we are but *whose* we are.[4]

What is this "word" we are called to share? It is a *personal* word which centers on what *Christ has done* . . . for *me*. Many groups have recognized that this witness has an inherent, repetitive structure to it and, having seen it, have

shared it with others in hopes of refining the witness borne.
The witness includes:

1. My life before Christ:

2. The context in which I accepted Christ:

3. My life since Christ became Lord:

   This is not to omit the testimonies of others or the Scriptures; indeed, they are our allies. But, they are just that—*our
allies*. One can share another's testimony and point to similar
biblical experiences and passages, but if *it has not come to
pass in one's own life,* all the testimonies in the world cannot suffice! We must learn that our testimony does not *back
up the Bible;* the Bible backs up our testimony! If this is not
so, then the Early Church could not have witnessed at all,
for the New Testament was not begun until twenty or thirty
years after Pentecost! This by no means depreciates the New
Testament, for it remains the "two-edged sword of the
Spirit," but the handle with which it is wielded is . . . *personal
testimony!*
   While some have an abhorrence to "plans of salvation,"

there is, nonetheless, a method to it. Once one begins to verbalize any process, it involves a structure or a plan. Salvation is no different. It has a process, a procedure, a plan. While no one "plan" encompasses the whole and while no "plan" can ever be valid apart from personal experience, there are several methods of presenting the gospel which have proved valuable to others. Until one is well-versed enough to devise his own personal approach, one would do well to implement one of the following—or something akin to them.

THE FOUR SPIRITUAL LAWS[5]

1. God *loves* you and has a *plan* for your life. (John 3:16; 10:10)
2. Man is *sinful* and *separated* from God, and thus cannot know His love and plan. (Romans 3:23; 6:23)
3. Jesus Christ is God's *only* provision for sin. Through Him we can know His love and plan. (Romans 5:8; John 14:6, II Corinthians 5:21)
4. We must *receive* Christ as Savior and Lord by personal invitation. (John 1:12; Rev. 3:20)

THE THREE S's OF SALVATION

1. Sin—Romans 3:23, Isaiah 53:6, I John 1:9
2. Savior—Isaiah 53:5, John 1:29
3. Surrender—John 1:12, Acts 16:31

THE ROMAN ROAD

Romans 3:23—All have sinned
Romans 6:23—The wages of sin: death
Romans 5:8—Christ paid the wages
Romans 10:9-13—Accept Christ as Savior

In summary, witnessing is sharing, out of experience, by life and by word, the Good News of Christ. It will implement the witness of the Bible and others. In the end, it points beyond oneself to the One who is the Explanation.

"I have encountered Him: He has reached me; He stood at my door and knocked, and, when I opened the door, He came in and communed with me."[6]

WHAT WITNESSING HAS BECOME. One does not have to be a student of the history of evangelism, however, to be aware that a shift in methods has taken place—somewhere between the first and twentieth centuries. One obvious shift is that from *personal* to *impersonal* evangelism. *Most* of the evangelism today has to do with mass, impersonal methods: radio, television, tracts and books and newspaper advertisements. Even much of the so-called "personal evangelism" allows one to "win" another and not even know his or her name!

No one has drawn a more satirical bead on impersonal evangelism than has Joseph Bayly in his *The Gospel Blimp.*[7] A church group, meeting in George and Ethel Griscom's backyard, became concerned about a beer-drinking neighbor and how he, and others like him, could be reached. Seeing a low-flying airplane, someone commented that it was too bad the plane did not carry a "Christian" sign so the neighbors could look up and see it. Out of it came the idea of a "gospel blimp," carrying a sign ("All have sinned") and dropping "gospel bombs"—tracts! Their idea was put into motion and the story grows more ludicrous, as you can imagine. Slowly, however, George and Ethel become disillusioned and drop out of the group. George is seen with the beer-drinking neighbor now quite frequently down at the bowling alley. How sad! The end, however, is that George at last invites the group over and there, to their amazement, is the neighbor; he has been won to Christ because George *personally* cared! Bayly concludes in his "interpretation" at the end of the book:

And the blimp? Why the wonderful Gospel Blimp is every impersonal, external means by which we try to fulfill our responsibility to witness to our neighbors. Gospel programs over the radio, messages on billboards or in tracts: these are some of our blimps. They either supplement our own personal witness or else they're substitutes for involvement with our neighbors—the sort of involvement that George and Ethel discovered toward the end of the story.[8]

A second obvious shift is that from *world-centered* to *church-centered* evangelism. Dr. Roy J. Fish, Professor of Evangelism at Southwestern Baptist Theological Seminary, has observed that we have changed the Great Commission from "Go and tell" to "Come and hear"! Mass evangelism, crusade evangelism, Sunday school evangelism, worship service evangelism—all say, "Come and hear." And it stands not only in contradistinction to Jesus' command, but to every method used by the early Christians!

Yet, when the Church is called to return to the *original*, it is viewed at best as *new* and, at worst, as *suspicious!* One hindrance to a return to New Testament evangelism is the obscuring fact that while *some* are won by these methods, *more* could be won by the original way! Somehow, we have allowed our methods to merge with our message until they are so completely identified that to question the *method* is to question the *message!*

But the fact is that in some quarters (and it is spreading), our methods are now failing. One church, which had depended for a generation on the evangelistic stand-bys of crusades and Sunday school, found itself stymied and without an evangelistic tool when both of these began to fall. (This is apparently not an isolated incident, if the reports from many quarters are true.) "Revivals" and Sunday school became the two lowest-attended programs! What were they to do? Re-emphasize "revivals" and Sunday school? Or, *evangelism?* Are they synonymous? Equally so, it is apparent that the present day evangelism explosion is taking place with other than traditional methods. The method and the message are not the same!

Church-centered, impersonal evangelism is winning some, but it has not proved adequate if our assignment, in fact, does include the world. It is not the better way because:

1. *It misses the masses.* The great masses of people do not, and will not, attend religious services of any kind. We often

miss this truth by viewing the crowds which do. Even city-wide and simultaneous church crusades indicate that the masses do not attend. If Gallup polls are any index, the problem has just begun! Even the fact that 2,000-member churches build auditoriums to seat 1,000 ought to be cause for alarm.

2. *It does not account for the societal changes taking place today.* Cosmopolitan living, and the anonymity it affords, has changed the picture altogether. The new style is characterized by the word "temporaneity." Over one half of the homes being built today are apartments! People are on the move—over half of the 885,000 listings in the Washington, D.C. telephone directory in 1969 were different in 1970! The new generation has *no ties*—especially "church ties"! And, while they do not have ties, they do have something else: *suspicions!* Apartment houses are guarded and apartment doors have chains—and both are used! Strangers, even Bible-toting ones, will not reach them! They will not/cannot be won by *any impersonal* means; *friends* alone will reach them —one-to-one, one-by-one.

3. *It does not fulfill the Great Commission.* Our abridged version of the Great Commission (Matthew 28:19-20) reads, "Go ye into all the world and make disciples . . ." (Thus endeth the reading!) A few Baptists and Disciples members add, "and baptize them . . ." and stop there. Jesus said, however, *"As ye go"* (literal Greek rendering); that is, evangelism is done in our *day-by-day activities.* He also added at the end of *our* conclusion, "and teach them to observe all the things I have commanded you." *Much* of contemporary evangelism does not fulfill His commission!

It is no harsh criticism to admit that much evangelism is akin to "scalp-hunting." It is quick, easy, simple, and . . . impersonal. "Do you believe this and this and this? Man, you're saved! Praise Jesus! By the way, what was your name again?" Sound familiar?

Somewhere, somehow we came to the conviction that salvation was something like a "spiritual vaccination"—a once-for-all, all-encompassing decision. "One shot'll do you!" Consequently, our evangelism has taken the shape of quick, easy decisions. Some hurriedly get their "converts" baptized. But the truth is, they are soon forgotten. Someone has said that the last instruction a new convert receives in most evangelical churches, after having come forward during an invitation, is to "fill out this card"! Evangelism intrinsically involves "teaching them to observe"—*or it is not evangelism!*

An all-important question is: what is the *object* of our witnessing to others? To save their souls? To get them to join the Church? To get them to accept Christ? To get them to be baptized? All of these have merit, but they are *secondary* goals at best. The object of witnessing is to . . . help others to become all that Christ wants them to be! These other things are but steps in the direction of that one final, ultimate goal. Christ has a plan for their lives; we are to help them find it!

If we are to win the masses, it will require new and/or better methods as well as an imperative.

WHAT WITNESSING MUST BECOME. If we are to reach out to others in the ultimate encounter anyone can make, at least two organizational things are imperative.[9]

First, the Church must provide *training*. Such training will begin with the cultivation of the Christ-life. (See Chapter Four.) It will go on, however, to the cultivation of the life of actual witness.

Two adequate illustrations are available to us: the Coral Ridge Presbyterian Church in Fort Lauderdale, Florida, and the First Baptist Church, Lake Jackson, Texas. One is situated in a growing metropolis and the latter in a medium-size city of 16,000. Both, however, are exploding churches—in evangelism. The secret in both instances is—intensive, pastor-led training. Not one-week courses, but months! In the case of the Coral Ridge Church it is six months; at Lake Jackson it is four months. The witnesses are trained. They go as silent observers for weeks into homes with witnessing sponsors. They report after each evening of visitation, and their strategy is analyzed and corrected. And it works! The First Baptist Church of Lake Jackson is reaching and baptizing and training over 200 each year! Coral Ridge grew from 0 to 2,000 members in nine years, from one minister to five, and to a peak attendance of 2,850 in four morning services![10]

Second, the Church must provide *channels* for witnessing. If the Gospel is to reach outside the four walls to the masses, two steps are involved. First, *target groups* must be established for witnessing. Where are the lost and forgotten masses? The addicts? The illiterates? The alcoholics? The non-church attenders? *Locate them!* Any church would profit by dismissing its regular services in an effort to see where the people are when the members are at church! They are in the bowling alleys, pool rooms, bars, backyards, and at the ball games. These must be reached and, if they are reached, they will be reached *where they are*. The second step is to organize (and train) *task groups* designed to involve themselves redemptively with the discovered *target groups*.[11]

The implementation of task groups remains as one of the most promising challenges to local congregations concerned about involved witnessing. While most churches have existing men's and women's organizations, these do not lend themselves to couples being involved together or to specific outreach ministries. By organizing small groups focused on specific tasks a church can afford many presently uninvolved adults with a channel of ministry. Also, such groups can study their task in an in-depth fashion. For instance, a group formed to minister to drug addicts can not only carry out their task, but can also study the nature of addiction as a part of the group function. Thus, their Christian education is correlated with their Christian service.

One church, built around renewal principles from its inception, requires new members to become immediately identified with one of their task groups. Their education then, in addition to the basic biblical studies, is specialized within that group's training program. Another church, having adopted the renewal concepts after years of existence, simply added a "Discipleship" section to the church's organizational structure. Directed by a coordinator, who is similar to a Sunday School Director, persons who want to become involved can be identified with a task group of their interest which offers training as part of the task. Other variations are available and the local situation will determine the nature and number of the groups. The challenge, however, remains with most local churches—to provide information on the target groups in need and the training for task groups to minister to them.

Reaching people is our *business!*

Witnessing is our *method!*

True, there may be no *wrong* way to witness, but there are *better* ways. We must learn them and then take the Word to *where the people are!*

Georges Bernanos, in his *Diary of a Country Priest,* has the "Judge" saying at the last day:

"*The word of God! Give me back my word!*"

And so it must be!

STUDY HELPS

Chapter Five

A. SMALL GROUP CREATIVE PROCEDURE

In advance, secure adequate copies of newspapers of recent date so that each person in the group may be given a complete edition. After distributing them, ask each person to recall a friend who is not a Christian and to have him in mind. Then provide fifteen minutes for each group member to tear from the pages headlines, articles, or advertisements in which their friend would be interested or which would cause worry or fear. These should be arranged on a place mat or a news sheet so they may be explained to the group.

Following this, the group is asked to discuss discovered similarities among unbelievers. What does this say to us about *how* we can and *why* we should be effective witnesses? Discuss the significance of the expression, "a life in which Christ is felt to live again." What qualities of life are most beneficial for a life of witness? What verbal forms would be valuable? What plans are we making to move ourselves toward these personal goals?

B.   For Further Reading

Urie Bender. *The Witness.* (Scottsdale, Pa.: Herald Press, 1965). Probably the most wholesome book on witnessing in print.

Leighton Ford. *The Christian Persuader.* (New York: Harper & Row, 1966).

James Kennedy. *Evangelism Explosion.* (Wheaton: Tyndale, 1970).

Ralph Neighbour, Jr. *Witness, Take the Stand.* (Published privately by the Baptist General Convention of Texas, Dallas, Texas).

Stephen F. Olford. *The Secret of Soulwinning.* (Chicago: Moody Press, 1963).

Bertha Smith. *Go Home and Tell.* (Nashville: Broadman, 1965).

Elton Trueblood. *The New Man for Our Time.* (New York: Harper & Row, 1970).

Chapter Six

A WORKING STRATEGY

To be on the road is not tantamount to arrival, but it is better than never starting.

We now have a view of a renewed church. It is the vision of a company of believers *all of whom* are ministers. They have heard a specific call to a particular ministry, and having heard, have prepared and involved themselves. They have a believing stance, a disciplined walk, and a witnessing life. What a vision! No one can begin to fathom the impact of such a group on a community!

But, *how?* How can a beginning be made? Of course, it would be convenient if such congregations could "start from scratch" with no traditions to hinder or chaff for the wind of the Spirit to drive away. Quite frankly, this has been the primary way in which renewal has taken place. And, sadly so. For it admits *a priori* that an existing congregation cannot make the transition. Indication from scattered quarters, however, is that it can! But, not with blood, sweat, toil, tears, and prayer![1] If renewal cannot come to an existing congregation, then it is not *renewal;* it is simply "new." We seek *renewal!*

AN EFFECTING STRATEGY. Our effecting strategy begins with two hard realizations. First, if renewal ever comes, it will be *via* a "church within the church." Such has existed all along; we simply have been too embarrassed to admit it. Jesus spoke of the wheat and tares growing up together and Calvin (rightly) believed that Christ meant the field to be the Church. That "church within the church" can be the saving salt. It is there that renewal will find fertile soil. Admit it and begin there!

Second, if the Church is to produce competent, disciplined ministers, we must be willing to admit that the existing educational and training structures will not suffice. It is not to say that they are not *good;* they are! They are just *not good enough.* Because they are mass-centered (toward large groups) and because the time allotted is so brief (one hour or less), they simply lack the dimension of depth. This dimension must be *added.* And it is here that some positive suggestions can be made.

Parallel Programs. Whatever renewal techniques have proved divisive in local churches, more often than not it has been due to over-zealous, well-meaning leaders attempting to "scrap" all of the existing programs at once. And—it fails every time! The answer lies in creating elective, parallel programs which supplement the existing programs with the dimension of depth. Through careful planning and cooperation, almost every church is open at this point.

By offering elective courses at the same time as Sunday school, Church Training programs, or mid-week services, those who want to go deeper may do so at no extra expense of time and scheduling. Also, those who desire to take such a course are usually eager enough to be willing to purchase the extra materials required.

In such a program, one church discovered that over a three-year period, they could offer Old Testament History, New Testament History, Theology, Ethics and Christian History—a basic foundation.[2] Specialized courses related to various outreach ministries can also be added. If a group is working with alcoholics, for instance, a course on the problem could be taught. The options to such are fantastic!

Special Programs. The church can also offer periodic special programs for a week, half-week, or a week-end. Many churches, having found "revivals" less and less effective as a method of evangelism, have simply filled the existing time-slots with new content. One church has instituted an annual Layman's Theological Seminar with a prominent theological personality leading it each year. Other possibilities are limitless: family life conferences, deeper life emphases, seminars on prayer or witnessing, in-depth Bible conferences, etc.

Small Groups. One of the most exciting discoveries of the last decade has been that of the small group. While there is danger in small groups (they can become divisive cliques), careful planning and coordination can overcome the problems and a tremendous force can be released. Any church desiring to use the small group concept would do well to preface the venture with an involved study of group dynamics and in the various possibilities for small group participation and activity.

Some helpful books on group dynamics are:

Groups Alive-Church Alive—Clyde Reid

Group Development—L. P. Bradford

Dare to Live Now!—Bruce Larson

Living on the Growing Edge—Bruce Larson

Also, suggestions for possible small group activities may be found in:

Spiritual Renewal Through Personal Groups—John Casteel

Group Dynamics in Evangelism—Paul M. Miller

Farewell to the Lonely Crowd—John W. Drakeford

Book Tables. One of the problems with church libraries is that no one uses them. Books, however, which are owned are something else. They can be studied, marked up, and referred to again. Yet, many persons who might otherwise read good books seldom enter bookstores. Why not set up a "book table" in the church? It has been done in many churches and with great success. Books may be secured from bookstores on consignment and can be sold at cost with little or no profit. Trueblood writes:

> Some, who now are serious about the universal ministry, can volunteer to conduct book tables within their church buildings, particularly on Sunday mornings. One who is willing to undertake this ministry can place a table in some part of the building, where people naturally pass by, and thus a wholly new group is reached. Curious as it may seem, not many people buy books or even know how to do so. There are large towns without bookstores and, though the denominational book services are active, people do not ordinarily buy books unless they actually see them in front of their eyes. To encourage people to buy is much better than to loan from a library, because then the book a man owns may be loaned to others. Furthermore he may mark it and thus make it truly his own.
>
> There need be no fear that the selling of books at church will introduce a jarring commercial note. There is nothing wrong with money, from a Christian point of view, especially when it is used to spread Christ's Kingdom. There is no difference, in principle, between the collection of money, in an offering, in order to spread the gospel to foreign lands and the collection of money from buyers of Christian books, in order to increase the spread of Christian ideas in the minds of the buyers. Both operations are part of the missionary enterprise. All suspicion of wrong motive can be allayed by carrying on the operation on a nonprofit basis. In any case, it is increasingly true that the steady operation of a book table, week after week, is one of the marks of a truly aroused church. The operation need not burden the pastor at all, and will not burden him, if some lay man or woman accepts the responsibility. Often willing people come to a pastor to ask for suggestions about what they can do. This is one.[3]

Retreats. Ultimately, however, the most productive technique remains the "retreat," the forty-four hour weekend beginning with the Friday evening meal. Because of the concentration possible and the away-from-home atmosphere, much can be learned and commitments can be made.

Retreats may take any number of forms, but the usual format is a combination of lectures, group discussion, and quiet times. Themes can include a wide variety of subjects. Those related to the renewal of the Church may focus on an over-all view of renewal (as with this book) or on a single aspect of it, i.e., the devotional life, witnessing, or doctrine. One error to be avoided is that of too wide a focus: *be specific* in your objective.

Those most knowledgable in the retreat concept agree that the idea of a pre-read, common textbook is of value in that it lends both a sense of direction and of community. Equally important to the success of a retreat (and success is best judged by the commitment achieved) is that of a commonly agreed "discipline" before and during the retreat, i.e., to read the book in advance, to attend the sessions, and to observe the quiet times. These two items are of tremendous importance: a common *goal* and a common *discipline* clearly understood by the participants.

One problem usually encountered at the very outset is where to hold the retreat: *a site*. The best, of course, is a retreat house designed for the purpose, such as the Yoke-fellow House in Richmond, Indiana, or Laity Lodge in Texas. These are rare, however, and while more are in the planning, other sites are most often used. Potential places are: Y.M.C.A. camps, Boy and Girl Scout camps, denominational camps, and the like. The best resource place is usually your local, regional, or state denominational office—most often, the Student Department. The one usual problem with these camps is that they are designed for children, not couples, and are dormitory style with large sleeping rooms. Very often, also, they do not provide cooks and table waiters or waitresses. No one in the retreat (ideally) should be involved in the preparation of meals, if possible: the retreat itself is of exclusive importance!

One scheduling problem with such camps is that they are designed for summer use only, prohibiting winter retreats while the summer is reserved for the regular camping program. Above all, get what you want and need in terms of facilities—even if some travel is involved. One hundred miles is a good outer limit if the retreat is to begin on a Friday night.

One, some, or all of these techniques may be the answer to your need. Others have found them immensely helpful in their working strategy of renewal.

At best, however, the above techniques are but "recovery" means. That is, their purpose is to regain the ground lost in the past generation. Of even greater importance is . . .

A CORRECTING STRATEGY. Parallel and special programs, seminars and retreats employed in renewal are often but efforts to reach those already or nearly lost to committed Christianity. Our *great* need is to reach the coming generations *before* . . . ! We need a permanent correcting strategy.

New Member's Classes. A good place to begin is with new converts and transfers. Russell Bow in his *The Integrity of Church Membership,*[4] reports some exciting and redemptive experiences with such an emphasis.

Tragically, most denominational literature for new members concentrates on the organizational structure of the denomination and the local church, and in the location of various denominational agencies. While such is valuable to intelligent churchmanship, what a new convert needs most to know is . . . how to pray and read his Bible, how to effect his witness, and how to assess the meaning of his new life in Christ!

Youth. What if our youth, our teenagers, could be taught renewal principles (the Universal Ministry, the life of discipline, etc.) *before* their adult years! These same techniques can be applied to their training as well, recognizing that the regular program is good, but not good enough. Most churches have long labored under the misconception that the way to enlist youth is to "entertain" them. This is obviously a misconception in that those churches with the largest and most effective youth programs are those which provide channels of service for their teens! The response to the Peace Corps and to other service-oriented youth groups serves as evidence that this generation of youth *wants to serve*, not to be served! The churches which provide opportunities and training will go a long way to insuring the renewal concepts for the future. The youth will entertain themselves; let them *serve—allow* them to serve!

Taxonomy. One great thing which remains in Christian education is . . . a taxonomy of studies in the Christ-life. This involves the correlation of educational steps in a progressing, step-by-step process. That is, we do not learn B until we learn A; we do not learn 3 times 2 is 6 until we learn simple addition. To date, there is relatively little attention given to this fundamental educational principle in Christian education. This means that what one now learns as a Beginner has no relationship to what he will learn as a Primary or Junior. Oh, for some local church committee, some denominational agency, to go to work on this crying need!

In conclusion, as one surveys the whole of renewal, the need and the consequent requirements, it is almost enough to make one wish he had been born into one of the vibrant hours of Christian history instead of this one. Yet, in every case, those bright hours came out of darkness similar to ours! In a very real sense Trueblood's aphorism is our only attitudinal approach: one is not responsible for the hand which is dealt to him, but only for how he plays it. *Our* hand is that self-same summons which came to Francis of Assisi:

RENEW MY CHURCH!

STUDY HELPS

Chapter Six

A.　SMALL GROUP CREATIVE PROCEDURE

Let the group list and discuss the potential need for a witnessing ministry in your community to:

1. Teenagers on drugs.
2. Divorcees.
3. Men who play golf every Sunday.
4. Unchurched children.
5. Habitual "week-enders," seldom in town on Sundays, such as campers and people who work on Sundays.
6. Proprietors of establishments selling alcoholic beverages.
7. Single young adults.
8. Any other "target groups" in your community.

What strategies would be effective in witnessing to all of these? How could you get such a set of strategies under way in your community? What training would be beneficial?

B. FOR FURTHER READING

Reports From Renewal Churches:

Russell Bow. *The Integrity of Church Membership.* (Waco: Word, 1968).

Robert E. Coleman. *Dry Bones Can Live Again.* (Old Tappan, N.J.: Revell, 1969).

Wallace Fisher. *From Tradition to Mission.* (Nashville: Abingdon, 1965).

————. *Preface to Parish Renewal.* (Nashville: Abingdon, 1968).

Ralph W. Neighbour, Jr. *The Seven Last Words of the Church.* (Grand Rapids: Zondervan, 1972).

Elizabeth O'Connor. *Call to Commitment.* (New York: Harper & Row, 1963).

Small Group Helps:

Philip A. Anderson. *Church Meetings That Matter.* (Philadelphia: United Church Press, 1965).

John L. Casteel. *Spiritual Renewal Through Personal Groups.* (New York: Association Press, 1967).

Clyde Reid. *Groups Alive—Church Alive.* (New York: Harper & Row, 1969).

Other Information:

Eric Hoffer. *The Ordeal of Change.* (New York: Harper & Row, 1952). A philosophical understanding of the mechanics of change.

Thomas J. Mullen. *The Dialogue Gap.* (Nashville: Abingdon, 1969).

Lyle E. Schaller. *The Impact of the Future.* (Nashville: Abingdon, 1969). A local church guide on changes the Church must make in our society.

Chapter Seven

AN EMPOWERING SPIRIT

Renewal begins on the inside.

A Catholic bishop has observed that all of the organizational changes taking place in the institutional church today are akin to "re-shuffling the deck chairs on the Titanic!" Apart from an empowering Spirit, he is correct! No matter how many organizational or structural changes, no matter how many innovations or new techniques—the renewal of the Church will not, *cannot*, come, apart from a Power beyond us. Someone related the story of the bush missionaries who had camped near a colony of monkeys for several days. Returning to the camp one day, they came upon the monkeys scurrying about in what was an obvious imitation of the missionaries! In the center of the camp, the monkeys had gathered firewood into a pile and were sitting around it as though warming themselves. They only lacked the fire! The Church is like that—with all of its changes and gathered sticks. Without the fire it is meaningless!

That fire is the Holy Spirit.

> "Not by might, nor by power, but by
> my Spirit, saith the Lord" (Zechariah 4:6).

Yet, among the most noticeable features of modern Christianity is the apparent absence of the Holy Spirit in the life of the Church and the believer, coupled with a more than apparent ignorance concerning His ministry! When these deficiencies are linked with the emphasis Jesus placed upon the absolute necessity of His ministry, it reveals—if nothing else—that the Holy Spirit is the overlooked option for modern Christianity! While we have tried to carry on without Him, Jesus stressed to His earlier disciples the impossibility of it! (Carl Bates says that the Holy Spirit could withdraw from the Church and ninety-five percent of our work would go on—and we would brag about its success!)[1]

As Jesus' earthly ministry began to draw to a close, He increasingly spoke of the coming ministry of the Holy Spirit. The evidence is that Jesus did not teach much at all about the Spirit in His earlier ministry. Yet a study of John's gospel (over half of which is devoted to the last week of Jesus' life), reveals Jesus' shift in emphasis. In that last week, every conversation, every prayer and every lesson inevitably led to the Spirit's pending ministry. (Begin with John 13:1 and study the references!) Jesus was simply re-stating the passage of Zechariah—and filling it with definitive content as to the who and what of the Spirit: *without Him you will be powerless!* (Acts 1:8)

There are many who point to the Resurrection as the stabilizing change in the life of the Church, saying that, until then, they were not stable. But, given the Resurrection, they were changed and en-nerved men. A study of the gospel accounts is helpful at this point for it reveals that this is not so! Even after the post-resurrection appearances, the disciples scattered and went back to their old vocations in an attitude of defeat and unconcern! (John 21). It was *Pentecost* which brought the change! *The coming of the Spirit!* There is the changing power! There alone! The Spirit alone is the answer to the phenomenal change and fantastic power of the Early Church. Those most studied in the book of Acts know full well that it is not the Acts of the *Apostles;* it is the

Acts of the Holy Spirit *in and through* the Apostles that we have recorded in the book!

If the Church is to be *renewed,* it will be renewed only by the Holy Spirit, not by techniques. "Renewal begins on the inside," in the spiritual life of the individual believers!

This is the *must* lesson of the Church today.

But, who is He and how does He work? While neither time nor space will permit a study of the Trinity and the full scope of the Spirit's ministry, suffice it that we focus on His *ministry to believers.* Indeed, the emphasis of the New Testament is just that; not His ministry to unbelievers (a common misunderstanding), but to . . . believers.

Two basic terms are used in the New Testament to describe the ministry of the Spirit to the followers of Christ. The first is . . .

THE INDWELLING OF THE HOLY SPIRIT

The "Indwelling" of the Holy Spirit refers to CONVERSION. While the death of our Lord provided the means to salvation, it is effected by the Holy Spirit—so taught Christ.

It is the Holy Spirit who convicts us of our need for salvation.

And when he comes, he will convince the world of sin and of righteousness and judgment. (John 16:8 RSV)

It is the Holy Spirit who regenerates us in salvation.

That which is born of the flesh is flesh, and that which is born of the Spirit is spirit. Do not marvel that I said to you, "You must be born anew." (John 3:6-7 RSV)

It is the Holy Spirit who takes up residence within us at conversion.

And I will pray the Father, and he will give you another Counselor, to be with you for ever, even the Spirit of truth, whom the world cannot receive, because it neither sees him nor knows him; you know him, for he dwells with you, and will be in you.   (John 14:16-17 RSV)

But ye are not in the flesh, but in the Spirit, if so be that the Spirit of God dwell in you. Now if any man have not the Spirit of Christ, he is none of his.   (Romans 8:9 KJV)

It is the Holy Spirit who seals us against the Day of Judgment, providing the earnest (the guarantee) of our eternal salvation.

In him you also, who have heard the word of truth, the gospel of your salvation, and have believed in him, were sealed with the promised Holy Spirit, which is the guarantee of our inheritance until we acquire possession of it, to the praise of his glory.   (Ephesians 1:13-14 RSV)

The second basic term used in the New Testament to describe His ministry to believers is . . .

THE INFILLING OF THE HOLY SPIRIT

The Infilling of the Holy Spirit refers to CONTROL. The key text for it is Ephesians 5:18.

And be not drunk with wine, wherein is excess; but be filled with the Spirit.   (Ephesians 5:18 KJV)

Notice carefully that Paul is drawing an analogy between alcoholic intoxication and control by the Holy Spirit. When one is "filled with wine" it does not mean that he is filled as is an empty vessel, from foot to head. Rather, it means that every part of his body is affected by the wine: how he walks, talks, thinks, and sees. So, too, with being "filled by Spirit"! It simply, but profoundly, means that our every action, thought and word is brought under His sway. To be "filled with the Spirit" refers to His taking control, mastering and possessing us.

A faulty conception of being Spirit-filled, however, is that this control is instantaneous (all at *once*) and instantaneously total (*all* at once). Contrary to such, it is not instantaneous just as being filled with wine is not. Rather, it is progressive, growing, and spreading in its effect, moving into every area of our lives.

The common biblical analogy of marriage and salvation is helpful at this point. Marriage requires but a simple act of commitment, yet the *implications* are profound! No one, at the time of marriage, knows fully the extent of the implications to saying "for better or for worse." But, they are saying in effect, "I am willing to accept the implications." Salvation (the acceptance of the *Lordship* of Christ) is a parallel. We do not fully grasp the implications of naming Jesus "Lord" of *every* area of our lives, but we accept the implications in full faith. Then, as in marriage, we spend our lives working out the implications of our commitment.

That it is not "automatic" is evidenced by Paul's own auto-biographical declaration to the Romans:

> I don't understand myself at all, for I really want to do what is right, but I can't. I do what I don't want to—what I hate. I know perfectly well that what I am doing is wrong, and my bad conscience proves that I agree with these laws I am breaking. But I can't help myself, because I'm no longer doing it. It is sin inside me that is stronger than I am that makes me do these evil things. I know I am rotten through and through so far as my old sinful nature is concerned. No matter which way I turn I can't make myself do right. I want to but I can't. When I want to do good, I don't; and when I try not to do wrong, I do it anyway. Now if I am doing what I don't want to, it is plain where the trouble is: sin still has me in its evil grasp. It seems to be a fact of life that when I want to do what is right, I inevitably do what is wrong. I love to do God's will so far as my new nature is concerned; but there is something else deep within me, in my lower nature, that is at war with my mind and wins the fight and makes me a slave to the sin that is still within me. In my mind I want to be God's willing servant but instead I find myself still enslaved to sin. So you see how it is: my new life tells me to do right, but the old nature that is still inside me loves to sin. Oh, what a terrible predicament I'm in! Who will free me from my slavery to this deadly lower

nature? Thank God! It has been done by Jesus Christ our
Lord. He has set me free.

(Romans 7:15-25 *Living Bible*)

In turn, Paul was to relate the meaning of this to the believers in the Galatian churches. He couched it in terms of a
battle within the heart of the Christians. The opposing sides
are "the flesh" and "the Spirit."

> *This* I say then, Walk in the Spirit, and ye shall not fulfill
> the lust of the flesh. For the flesh lusteth against the Spirit,
> and the Spirit against the flesh: and these are contrary the
> one to the other: so that ye cannot do the things that ye
> would. But if ye be led of the Spirit, ye are not under the
> law. Now the works of the flesh are manifest, which are
> *these*: Adultery, fornication, uncleanness, lasciviousness,
> Idolatry, witchcraft, hatred, variance, emulations, wrath,
> strife, seditions, heresies, Envyings, murders, drunkenness,
> revellings, and such like: of the which I tell you before, as I
> have also told *you* in time past, that which do such things
> shall not inherit the kingdom of God. But the fruit of the
> Spirit is love, joy, peace, longsuffering, gentleness, goodness,
> faith, Meekness, temperance: against such there is no law.
> And they that are Christ's have crucified the flesh with the
> affections and lusts.   (Galatians 5:16-24 KJV)

Walking in the flesh and walking in the Spirit are two ir-
reconcilable ways of life. As one lusts (fights) against the
other, the human heart becomes a veritable battleground.
The "flesh" seeks to produce the works of the flesh, and Paul
lists them for us. The Spirit, however, seeks to produce those
Christ-like qualities which Paul calls "the fruits of the Spirit."
And the battle rages!

The presence of those "fruits" constitutes the Spirit-filled
(controlled) life. As He conquers the flesh, the fruits begin
to appear—not instantaneously or simultaneously, but *pro-
gressively*. They are *His* fruits; He produces them as we yield
control to Him. He *will* produce in us: love, joy, peace, pa-
tience, kindness, goodness, faithfulness, gentleness and self-
control.

Other scriptural promises about the Spirit's workings are equally important.

He *teaches:*

> But as it is written, Eye hath not seen, nor ear heard, neither have entered into the heart of man, the things which God hath prepared for them that love him. But God hath revealed *them* unto us by his Spirit: for the Spirit searcheth all things, yea, the deep things of God.
>
> (I Corinthians 2:9-10 KJV)

He *leads:*

> For all who are led by the Spirit of God are sons of God.
>
> (Romans 8:14 RSV)

He *assures:*

> It is the Spirit himself bearing witness with our spirit that we are children of God. (Romans 8:16 RSV)

He *empowers* for witnessing:

> But you shall receive power when the Holy Spirit has come upon you; and you shall be my witnesses in Jerusalem and in all Judea and Samaria and to the end of the earth.
>
> (Acts 1:8 RSV)

He *strengthens:*

> That he would grant you, according to the riches of his glory, to be strengthened with might by his Spirit in the inner man. (Ephesians 3:16 KJV)

Do you see it? *The goals of renewal and the fruits of the Spirit are one and the same!* There is the answer to power beyond us to accomplish. They are *His fruits,* He *alone* can produce them!

The "How" of Spirit-Control

While there is always a danger in simple formulas in spiritual matters, there is scriptural evidence that a pattern for personal, spiritual renewal exists. At least five elements are involved in the "how."

Decisively. The move to a Spirit-controlled life is as much a decision as is conversion itself. This is not to say that the Holy Spirit is not permanently and fully present from the moment of conversion, for He is. You now have all of the Spirit that there is—if you are a Christian. It is, however, to admit that there is a vast difference in saying you have all of the Spirit and in saying the Spirit has all of you! Therein lies the problem!

Dr. Ralph Herring illustrates this so clearly in a brilliant anecdote:

> Many years ago there was to be a wedding between two very prominent families. Wealth and social distinction were on both sides of the match, and it was natural that the event should assume proportions of the first magnitude. Elaborate preparations were made. The minister who was to perform the ceremony and his wife were greatly interested, of course, and would have been less than human if they had not speculated between themselves what the fee might be. Maybe the minister's wife, who according to a custom of long standing lays claim to the wedding fee, was thinking in terms of a new bonnet!
>
> However, when the ceremony was over the groom presented the minister with a pair of kid gloves as a token of his appreciation. The preacher took them home, and with a laugh tossed them into his wife's lap saying, "There's your wedding fee." They laughed together, for obviously the gloves were too large for her and he was not the glove-wearing kind. Thus, the incident passed.
>
> Some months later, however, as he was packing for a trip, his wife suggested that he ought to take the gloves. He might want to wear them amid his new surroundings. Thinking well of the idea he tried them on for the first time. To his surprise he found something lodged in one of the fingers

of the glove. Pulling it out, he discovered a neatly folded ten-dollar bill. In the second finger he found another. Then excitedly he and his wife went through the fingers and thumbs of the gloves, finding in each a crisp ten-dollar bill —a handsome fee of one hundred dollars.[2]

You see, he had it all along! It was just undiscovered and unappropriated!

The Spirit's ministry is put into effect when we deliberately decide to give Him *full* control in a decisional fashion. It is to say with St. Francis de Sales: *"Yes, God, yes, and always yes!"*

Daily. The Spirit-filled life, like conversion, is not meant to be a one-time, all-encompassing event like a "spiritual vaccination." It is continuously done, day by day. Jesus said we are to "take up our crosses *daily*"[3] and—crosses are to die on! Daily we are to be dying to self and yielding to the Spirit.

Every morning should find the believer dressed in his shroud and reporting for duty!

Devotionally. Those whose Spirit-walk we most admire are unanimous in one thing: there is no deep, power-filled spiritual life apart from a rich devotional life. (See Chapter Four). Bible study, devotional reading, spoken and meditative prayer, studies in the lives of great saints—are as necessary to spiritual life as milk to babies and air to the lungs.

The Spirit-filled life is born and nurtured in the context of a devotional life.

Doubtlessly. While every promise of the Holy Spirit made by Jesus was actualized on the Day of Pentecost (Acts 2), while the Scriptures abound with assured claims concerning His ability, and while the accumulated testimony across the two thousand years of Christian history has repeatedly verified it—we still have a tendency to doubt that He can do it *for us!* The only way to face the possibility of a Spirit-controlled life is with faith. *I believe!*

Faith (which is simply "confidence in Christ") grows as it is used. This is evidenced by our faith in others. We "try" a person once and, when he proves trustworthy and true to his word, we are more willing to trust him the next time. So, too, with Christ. Start where you are with whatever faith you have. Use it and it will grow. The place to begin is with the faith that Christ has *promised* us certain things in regard to the Holy Spirit. Believe *Him!*

However, it is critically important to understand the difference between *faith* and *feeling*. The Holy Spirit is not affected or changed by our feelings at the moment! He is *always* at work in us, whether we "feel" it or not. There is no biblical evidence, *none whatsoever*, that we can "feel" the Spirit—some old Negro "spirituals" perhaps, but nothing in the Scriptures! The Apostle John gave us a great promise when he wrote: "If our heart condemn us, God is greater than our hearts" (I John 3:20)! And, he adds: "Greater is he (the Spirit) that is in you than he (the Devil) that is in the world" (I John 4:4). *Believe!*

Discoveringly. Finally, we walk in the Spirit discoveringly. As we yield day by day, and moment by moment, the Spirit has a way of opening new doors of exciting opportunities to us. Whatever the Spirit-filled life is, it is not dull!

Paul gave us the pattern in Romans 6:

> Do not yield your members to sin as instruments of wickedness, but yield yourselves to God as men who have been brought from death to life, and your members to God as instruments of righteousness.   (Romans 6:13 RSV)

First, *yield yourself*—initially, totally and committedly. Then, begin to *yield your members*—step by step as the Spirit points up the need.

Dr. Ralph Neighbour has an exacting analogy for us. Dr. Neighbour says that the common conception of the Christian is like a person walking up onto the porch of a large, dark house. Looking for the lights, he gropes about on the porch until he finds the control box and, pulling the switch, every light in the house goes on! *But*, he goes on, *that is not how it works!*

Rather, one finds the box, throws the switch and . . . *one tiny light* just over his head comes on! One tiny light! It gives him only enough light to enter and to see the hall switch.

And we spend the rest of our Christian lives going from new room to new room, throwing the switches and discovering new and unexplored corners to our lives! *Discoveringly!*

In conclusion, no amount of stress is sufficient to adequately impress the absolute necessity of personal, spiritual renewal *preceding* church renewal. It is said that Lawrence of Arabia came to London once, following his exciting military life, and brought with him a number of Arab chieftains. It was their first trip outside the deserts and, needless to say, they were over-awed with the city. They were most impressed, however, with the water faucets in the hotel rooms! Coming from the barren, waterless deserts, it was fantastic to them that simply by turning a handle *at any time* water would pour out! The report is that after they departed, the hotel management made an unusual discovery: the water faucets had all been removed! The Arabs had taken them! They thought, you see, that they could take them back to the desert, turn the handle, and water would pour forth. How absurd! The faucets were not connected to the water supply.

Just as absurd is the Christian who believes he can produce the Christ-like qualities apart from being controlled by the Spirit!

There is no possibility apart from Him for renewal! Thus the call to *Renew My Church!* is predicated on the prayer: *Renew My Heart!*

STUDY HELPS

Chapter Seven

A. SMALL GROUP CREATIVE PROCEDURE

The group, having shared together thus far, must now come first to personal and then to corporate commitment. Provide an "Hour of Silence," during which each individual is to find a very private place for self-examination. There should be absolutely no verbal communication during this hour! The following material is to be used individually during this time.

Unless one has experienced the meaning of the Spirit-filled life, renewal is impossible. The key to this experience is in John 7:37-38. The process is to admit to one's self:

1. *I am thirsty.* My life is like a desert. I have lost my first love. I possess a deep inner longing for God's life to flow through mine.

2. *I must be cleansed.* I cannot expect God to put His Holy Spirit in an unholy life. I will list my sins, known and unconfessed, on a sheet of paper. I will deal with them according to the teaching in I John 1:9. I will acknowledge to others, where necessary, my wrong spirit.

3. *I must present myself* to the Lord Jesus Christ as one ready to be totally and completely filled with His divine plans. I will, in prayer, "choose God's will in the place of my will in every situation."

4. *I will then remain* in a spirit of continuing confession of sins and accepting the death of my self-life. I will continually be in the process of receiving the life of the Holy Spirit in the place of my own selfish life. I will "count on it as a continuing fact"—Christ lives in me, and I no longer express my wishes in conflict with His.

5. *In obedience* which is single-minded, I will do His will regardless of personal sacrifice or discipline required. I will share with Him my love and demonstrate His life through absolute submission to Him.

Before returning to the group, position yourself in these terms with God through prayer. How near or far are you from this covenant?

Following the "Hour of Silence," each person is to be given freedom to present to the group a Statement of Pilgrimage, outlining precisely where he is in the matter of accepting the discipline of the Spirit-filled life.

(If the group is not on a retreat, but is meeting as a periodic study group, the above may be done privately before the meeting. The "Statement of Pilgrimage" can be used, however, in a group meeting or on a retreat.)

Following this, the groups should close with corporate prayer. "Conversational prayer" is most appropriate for this. Perhaps an expression of involvement in ministry may follow this before dismissal.

B. For Further Reading

Biblical Perspective:

J. Sidlow Baxter. *Going Deeper*. (Grand Rapids: Zondervan, 1962).

F. J. Huegel. *Bone of My Bone*. (Grand Rapids: Zondervan, 1940).

John Hunter. *Knowing God's Secrets*. (Grand Rapids, Zondervan, 1965).

L. E. Maxwell. *Born Crucified*. (Chicago: Moody, 1945).

Ruth Paxson. *Life on the Highest Plane*. (Chicago: Moody, 1928). The classic on the Spirit-filled life.

Samuel Shoemaker. *With the Holy Spirit and Fire*. (New York: Harper & Row, 1960).

Jack R. Taylor. *The Key to Triumphant Living*. (Nashville: Broadman, 1971).

Ian Thomas. *The Mystery of Godliness*. (Grand Rapids: Zondervan, 1964).

————. *The Saving Life of Christ*. (Grand Rapids: Zondervan, 1961). Considered Thomas' best book on the deeper life.

Personal Perspective:

Dietrich Bonhoeffer. *The Cost of Discipleship*. (New York: Macmillan, 1963). Must reading for committed Christians today.

V. Raymond Edman. *They Found the Secret*. (Grand Rapids: Zondervan, 1960). Personal stories of the deeper life.

Samuel Shoemaker. *Extraordinary Living for Ordinary Men.* (Grand Rapids: Zondervan, 1965).

Douglas Steere. *On Beginning From Within.* (New York: Harper & Row, 1964).

FOOTNOTES

Chapter One

1 Elton Trueblood. *Company of the Committed.* (New York: Harper and Row, 1961). pp. 2-4.
2 Karl Heim. *Christian Faith and Natural Science.* (New York: Harper and Brothers, 1957). p. 24.
3 Colin Morris. *Include Me Out.* (Nashville: Abingdon, 1968). pp. 7-9.
4 Elton Trueblood. *Op. Cit.* p. 9.
5 Keith Miller. *The Taste of New Wine* (1965) and *A Second Touch* (1967). (Waco: Word Books).
6 See: Elizabeth O'Connor. *Call to Commitment.* (New York: Harper and Row, 1963) for the story of the "Church of the Savior" in Washington, D.C.; Ralph W. Neighbour. *The Seven Last Words of the Church.* (Grand Rapids: Zondervan, 1972) for the story of the "Touch" ministries at West Memorial Baptist Church in Houston; and Wallace Fisher. *From Tradition to Mission.* (Nashville: Abingdon, 1965).
7 Thomas J. Mullen. *The Ghetto of Indifference.* (Nashville: Abingdon, 1966). pp. 38-39.
8 Thomas J. Mullen. *The Renewal of the Ministry.* (Nashville: Abingdon, 1963). p. 140.

Chapter Two

1 See: Francis O. Ayres. *The Ministry of the Laity.* (Philadelphia: Westminster, 1961); Robert Raines. *New Life in The Church.* (New York: Harper and Row, 1961); Elton Trueblood. *Op. Cit.*
2 Elton Trueblood. *Op. Cit.* p. 60.
3 Francis O. Ayres. *Op. Cit.* p. 31.

4 Robert Raines. *Op. Cit.* p. 17.
5 Thomas J. Mullen. *The Renewal of the Ministry.*
6 Elton Trueblood. *The Incendiary Fellowship.* (New York: Harper and Row, 1965). p. 53.

Chapter Three

1 "Faith" is understood in two ways: as a body of doctrine and as personal trust. Throughout this chapter it is used in the former sense.
2 This is a good discussion point for a group or retreat.
3 Elton Trueblood. *A Place to Stand.* (New York: Harper and Row, 1969).
4 Dictionaries: *Smith's Bible Dictionary, The Zondervan Pictorial Bible Dictionary,* or *Peloubet's Bible Dictionary.* Word Books: *A Theological Wordbook* (Richardson, ed.) or *A Companion to the Bible* (Von Allmen, ed.). Commentaries: *Commentary on the Whole Bible* (Jamieson, Fausset, Brown), *Ellicott's Bible Commentary* (Zondervan) or *The Wycliffe Bible Commentary.* These, and other good volumes, are available in religious bookstores.
5 Carlyle Marney. *The Coming Faith.* (Nashville: Abingdon, 1970). p. 168.

Chapter Four

1 Douglas Steere. *On Beginning From Within.* (New York: Harper and Row, 1964). p. 41.
2 E. Herman. *Creative Prayer.* (New York: Harpers, 1934). p. 28.
3 Thomas R. Kelly. *A Testament of Devotion.* (New York: Harper and Row, 1941). pp. 45-46.
4 Elton Trueblood. *The Life We Prize.* (New York: Harper and Row, 1951). pp. 200-201.
5 These are printed by several publishers and may be secured in almost any bookstore.
6 L. E. Maxwell. *Born Crucified.* (Chicago: Moody Press, 1945); F. J. Huegel. *Bone of His Bone.* (Grand Rapids: Zondervan, 1940).

Chapter Five

1 Elton Trueblood. *Company of the Committed.* pp. 68-69.
2 From *The Witness* by Urie A. Bender. Copyright © 1965 by Herald Press, Scottsdale, Pa. 15683, pp. 42-43. Used by permission. This is one of the best books on witnessing in print today!

3 *Ibid.* p. 43.

4 Trueblood. *Company of the Committed.* pp. 53-54.

5 Printed by permission. © 1965 by *Campus Crusade for Christ, Inc.* All rights reserved. The following is a suggested prayer to go with these four spiritual laws:
"Lord Jesus, I need You. I open the door of my life and receive You as my Savior and Lord. Thank You for forgiving my sins. Take control of the throne of my life. Make me the kind of person You want me to be."

6 Trueblood. *Company of the Committed.* p. 50.

7 Joseph Bayly. *The Gospel Blimp.* (Grand Rapids: Zondervan, 1960). This has since been made into a motion picture.

8 *Ibid.* p. 77.

9 Of prior importance is a clear understanding that there can be no effective witnessing done apart from a Christ-controlled life. (Chapter 7.) Dr. Neighbour says: "I am coming to an ever-growing realization that the first step in witnessing must be the personal, total abandonment to the Lordship of Christ. In retrospect, I can think of not one effective person in the field of personal witnessing who has not first discovered the secret of the Christ-filled life."

10 See: D. James Kennedy. *Evangelism Explosion.* (Wheaton: Tyndale, 1970). This is the story of the Coral Ridge Church.

11. See: Ralph W. Neighbour. *The Seven Last Words.*

Chapter Six

1 See: Keith Miller's *A Taste of New Wine,* chapter 9; and *A Second Touch,* chapters 10-14.

2 Elizabeth O'Connor's *Call to Commitment* offers such a suggested curriculum as does Elton Trueblood in his *Your Other Vocation* (New York: Harper and Row, 1952). pp. 106-125.

3 Elton Trueblood. *The Yoke of Christ.* (New York: Harper and Row, 1958). p. 142.

4 Russell Bow. *The Integrity of Church Membership.* (Waco: Word Books, 1968).

Chapter Seven

1 This reference is made in a truly significant book on the Holy Spirit: Samuel Shoemaker. *With the Holy Spirit and With Fire.* (New York: Harper and Row, 1960).

2 Ralph A. Herring. *God Being My Helper.* (Nashville: Broadman, 1955). pp. 137-138.

3 Luke 9:23. See: L. E. Maxwell. *Op. Cit.*